ALSO BY WILLIAM GILDEA

*When the Colts Belonged to Baltimore: A Father and a Son,
a Team and a Time*

*Where the Game Matters Most: A Last Championship
Season in Indiana High School Basketball*

THE
LONGEST
FIGHT

THE LONGEST FIGHT

In the Ring with Joe Gans, Boxing's

First African American Champion

WILLIAM GILDEA

Farrar, Straus and Giroux   New York

Farrar, Straus and Giroux
18 West 18th Street, New York 10011

Grateful acknowledgment is made for permission to reprint the following previously published material:

Quotations from the writings of H. L. Mencken, published by permission of the Enoch Pratt Free Library, Baltimore, in accordance with the terms of Mr. Mencken's will and his bequest to the Library.

Passage by David Halberstam from the book *ESPN SportsCentury*, edited by Michael MacCambridge, foreword by Chris Berman, and introduction by David Halberstam. Copyright © 1999 by ESPN, Inc. Reprinted by permission of Hyperion. All rights reserved.

Lines from "The Time of Ruby Robert" by Edgar Lee Masters, published in *Esquire*, February, 1940. Reprinted by permission of Hilary Masters.

Excerpt from *Invisible Man* by Ralph Ellison. Copyright 1947, 1948, 1952 by Ralph Ellison. Copyright renewed © 1975, 1976, 1980 by Ralph Ellison. Used by permission of Random House, Inc.

Lyrics from "George Jones," from *Songs of Yale*. Composed by Marshall Bartholomew. Copyright © 1934 (Renewed) by G. Schirmer, Inc. (ASCAP). International Copyright Secured. All Rights Reserved. Used by Permission.

Library of Congress Cataloging-in-Publication Data
Gildea, William.
  The longest fight : in the ring with Joe Gans, boxing's first African American champion / William Gildea. — 1st ed.
    p.   cm.
  Includes bibliographical references and index.
  ISBN 978-0-374-28097-0 (alk. paper)
  1. Gans, Joe. 2. Boxers (Sports)—United States—Biography.
  3. African American boxers—Biography. I. Title.

GV1132.G33G55 2012
796.83092—dc23
[B]

2011040170

Designed by Jonathan D. Lippincott

www.fsgbooks.com

1   3   5   7   9   10   8   6   4   2

Frontispiece: Joe Gans in August 1906, in Goldfield, Nevada, before his fight with Battling Nelson (The Gary Schultz Collection)

FOR MARY FRAN

CONTENTS

THE
LONGEST
FIGHT

PROLOGUE

There's always something more to the finding in the Library of Congress. Going there is about possibilities. You don't quite know where to look, what building to go to, what door to go through, what shelf to climb up to, what drawer to pull open, whom to ask. But then one day, quite by accident, you wander down a narrow carpeted hallway, and sitting behind a mahogany divider is research librarian Dave Kelly, and late in the conversation he casually says, *Well, there is some film of Joe Gans.* He believes it's of a fight in 1906 with Battling Nelson. He tells me to go across the street and try the Motion Picture and Television Reading Room, part of the Motion Picture, Broadcasting, and Recorded Sound Division, in the Madison Building, second floor.

Gans was the first African American boxing champion. Parts of his repertoire were copied by the likes of Jack Johnson, Joe Louis, the young Muhammad Ali, and the young Mike Tyson. Gans, the lightweight champion from 1902 to 1908, perfected modern boxing; he was that significant a figure.

But his achievements in the ring are not foremost in this story. They frame the story. The heart of it is this: what it was like a century ago to be black in America, to be a black boxer, to be the first black athlete to successfully cross the nation's gaping racial divide, to give early-twentieth-century African Americans hope, a word we hear so often today.

Some realms of Gans's story are wrapped in thick mist—his

parents, his childhood, his first love. Others are clear enough: The discrimination he faced as an African American—as David Remnick has written, boxing's subtext has always been America's subtext, race; the crossover appeal he gained among whites that, in particular, Joe Louis and Jesse Owens would win three decades later to (understandably) a far greater degree, when they triumphed against a backdrop of Nazism; the inseparability of Gans's success in the ring and the constraints he faced, unfairness that sometimes waylaid him but never stopped him. The success and the discrimination are forever intertwined.

Still other parts of his life, it turns out, are recorded in amazing detail, such as the film of his fight to the finish with Battling Nelson in that time-stilled eternity under the blistering sun of the Nevada desert, in the twentieth century's longest championship fight. The other fight goes on longer; it's easier to change the language of a century ago, but it remains harder to win hearts. A century ago one could barely conceive of a black man establishing himself as the best in any walk of life, but here's one man's quest, hiding almost in plain sight, in two bulky gray canisters with the film inside.

In a darkened back room, a librarian cues them up, first one then the other, and it takes almost three hours to watch, just about the time it took for the fighters to fight, and thus are verified the blow-by-blow descriptions that newspapers printed in that era. Later, facing a computer, you combine the blur of Gans's life more than a century ago with him under the microscope of the film.

Battles had previously transpired: Napoleon's, Alexander's, Hector's, Ramses', Jacob's with the angel—but here, for one of the first times, you can see what's happening and know how boxing came to mean big money: Gans and Nelson and their suffering, the men in the ring's corners holding up umbrellas to shield the fighters from a desert afternoon's unrelenting sun, spectators in the stands surrounding the ring. How did they reach there? By horse, mostly. Their shirts are white and pressed and they wear ties and hats with handkerchiefs draped down the back to protect their necks from the sun. The film jerks the context out of the people and the place and nails them to now.

PART ONE

If the Civil War had been fought to end slavery, then there was in the Reconstruction era, as the true political price of reunion emerged, a resurgence of racism, slavery replaced by legal racism, and fierce continued suppression of the children of slaves . . . In the new century, one of the great struggles played out would be that of black Americans struggling for full citizenship. And no arena would show-case this battle in a series of stunning and often bitterly divisive increments, or reflect the true talents of black America more clearly, than the world of sports.

—David Halberstam, "A Dynasty in the Making," introduction to ESPN SportsCentury, 1999

1

He had an unmarked face except for a modest scar above the outer corner of each eye and a small amount of puffiness below the left—remarkable for someone approaching, at minimum, his 187th professional prizefight. He was trim, with broad, sloping shoulders, but stood just 5 feet 6½ inches and weighed about 140 pounds. A photograph of him taken in 1906 shows him shirtless, arms folded across his midsection, his upper body spectacularly muscled.

One August evening that year, Joe Gans rode a train deep into the Nevada desert. The newly built rail line extended south for twenty-six miles, the brief last leg of a trip that had taken him from San Francisco's East Bay up the mountains to Reno, then to a seemingly endless journey to Tonopah, Nevada, and on toward a mining boomtown called Goldfield. A group of settlers had named it three years earlier after prospectors had come upon yellowed rocks that held the promise of a great gold strike.

In thirteen years as a professional boxer, Gans had crossed the country several times by train. On different occasions he had traveled from the East Coast to fight in Oregon, San Francisco, Los Angeles, and Seattle. He had seen the desert. But it had never been his destination. And it never would have been except that he, like the prospectors aboard the train, was being lured across a wilderness of sand and sagebrush by a quest for wealth. They went for the gold. He went for the payday that came with defending his world lightweight championship. His glories in the ring notwithstanding, he was virtually broke.

The newspapers were predicting an epic encounter between him and Battling Nelson, a fighter succinctly and gruesomely described by Jack London as "the abysmal brute." Gans and Nelson would meet on Labor Day afternoon, under the desert sun. There would be no scheduled end to the fight. It would be a fight to the finish, usually when one man dropped and stayed down until the count of ten. Fights with no prescribed end could feel, to a fighter, like an eternity. They left most scarred. More than once, a manager threw a towel into the ring because he had no doubt that the next blow would leave his fighter dead. Sometimes the towel landed too late.

Gans anticipated danger. It came with his business and his skin color. He was the first black American boxing champion, but that achievement brought him more peril than renown. The discrimination that black boxers faced reflected American life. In 1906 racial injustice was far worse than it had been three and a half decades earlier when Walt Whitman recognized the separation of races as one of the flaws that made the country's future "as dark as it is vast." Gans had received death threats throughout his career, and he wouldn't be surprised to hear from someone betting for or against him at Goldfield that he had better win or lose as directed or risk not getting out of town alive.

No entourage accompanied him aboard the Tonopah and Goldfield train. It wasn't his style to make himself the center of attention, even if a black man dared to. He passed the time in thought, knowing that trouble was coming, merely unsure what form it would take. Only recently—quite belatedly, out of misplaced loyalty—had he fired his manager, Abraham Lincoln Herford, known as Al. For years, this burly, cigar-smoking white man had treated him as a serf, pocketing most of his earnings while posing as his best hope.

What little Herford left him, Gans gambled away. He was bad at picking winners at the racetrack, and he was a loser at cards and dice. He always kept enough money, however, to maintain a fine wardrobe. He wore three-piece suits with a handkerchief jutting from the breast pocket, white shirts with starched collars, a diamond stickpin, a loop of gold watch chain across his chest, and a derby when he stepped out at night. One of his outfits was especially celebratory: a pale green suit, Alice blue socks, and yellow shoes. Daytimes, he preferred turtleneck jerseys or sweaters, slacks, and a cap.

Appearances aside, Gans was as poor in 1906 as in 1896, when he emerged from his native Baltimore to seek the lightweight championship. If the heavyweight division was boxing's most prestigious, the lightweight ranks were its most competitive. A boxer could make good money as a lightweight. The division was filled with great fighters, and almost every one was vicious and unforgiving. Nelson, born in Copenhagen and nicknamed "the Durable Dane," was a brawler who could withstand the hardest punches. If knocked down, he could be counted on to get up and keep swinging as though he hadn't been touched. He hit below the belt, he held and hit, and he gouged eyes. There wasn't a dirty tactic that he hadn't tried.

Like prospectors out for gold, Gans would work with his hands, and his work, like theirs, would take time. It might punish and discourage him. The desert fed discouragement. So did Nelson, who was twenty-four and in his fighting prime.

Gans was thirty-one. He had been boxing almost half his life, and there were indications that his best days in the ring had passed. As he sought a divorce the previous year, *The Washington Post* paraphrased his testimony in Baltimore's Circuit Court No. 2, saying that even Gans himself believed "the zenith of his success had been reached and that he was now on the backward track . . . that he was about all in as a professional scrapper."

Gans's wife demanded $200 to cover her lawyer's fee and $25 a week in alimony pending the outcome of his suit. Gans explained that he was not only broke but also in debt to Herford for thousands of dollars with little hope of repaying him. No one could say that he was exaggerating his decline as a boxer and his capacity for earning money in the future, including the presiding judge, who awarded Gans's wife a customary $25 for her lawyer's work and $5 a week in alimony pending the court's decision.

Herford had a reputation for paying his fighters next to nothing.

Boxing was a bettor's province, and for years Herford had raked in money by betting heavily on Gans—not only *that* he would win, but *when* he would win—in what round. He often arranged to have Gans go easy on white fighters, enabling them to last a respectable amount of time so as not to embarrass them too badly. Gans had the talent to score a knockout in the round Herford ordained—and bet on. When Herford let him fight without restrictions, he was practically invincible. In time, Herford found fewer and fewer takers for his bets; almost no one wanted to bet against Gans. So he persuaded Gans to lose intentionally. One effect of this was to take money out of the pockets of poor blacks who bet on Gans religiously—and the thought tormented him. Six months before his trip into the desert, he admitted his folly to a newspaper reporter and vowed to fight honestly every time. Leaving Herford behind, Gans headed to Goldfield nagged by regret.

2

Goldfield is situated in remote south central Nevada, on a large plain more than a mile high at the base of the pyramidal Columbia Mountain. In 1906, it was reachable by car, but only the occasional wealthy person had one. And only a minority of those who worked in the mines had the train fare. Most made it by horse-drawn wagon or on the back of a horse or burro. Some men took their wives and children, forming caravans of buckboards. Others walked empty-handed.

If the land didn't get them, the weather might. They could be obliterated by the wind and blinded by sandstorms or stuck when rain turned the dust to mud and their wagon wheels sank. In the summer, described by one visitor as "Dante's Inferno with the lid off," many were victimized by dehydration and hallucinations. In winter, they might face misery as their open stagecoach inched through sleet and slush at four miles an hour, or they could be halted by snowdrifts or killed by the cold.

"Goldfield is a sadly hideous aggregation of tents, huts, shacks, adobes, frame houses, and three good stone buildings," Parmeter Kent remarked in 1906 in the first issue of his monthly, the *Goldfield Gossip*, ten cents a copy. "The climate is, perhaps, the worst in the world. For three months it scorches the life out of you; freezes and chills you for another three, and blows what's left of you into dust for the remaining six . . . Goldfield is not a health resort. It is not beautiful. But it is the greatest spot on earth to make money, and that is what we are here for."

Kent was there to make money in publishing. In reality he was Sidney Flower, who took off for Goldfield after a magazine he owned in Chicago had been shut down for mail fraud. By 1906, fifteen to twenty thousand people had settled there. They had come from all over North America, from Mexico and Peru, from England and South Africa and Australia, all determined to reach this obscure speck of land that would become America's last mining boomtown. They hoped to hit the biggest bonanza since the Comstock Lode in western Nevada more than a quarter century earlier. They took a chance, and Gans took a chance as well. Neither he nor Nelson had signed a contract, although that didn't mean much to Gans. Even when he was champion, his race forbade him to dictate terms, and he had wired the promoter accepting the fight not knowing how the money would be split. He neared Goldfield knowing that a fight with Nelson would be the most important of his life, and he was willing to compromise in the arrangements to ensure it took place.

The train pulled into town in the dark. It was 9:15 p.m. on August 7 when he alighted into a crowd of miners gathered at the depot—grizzled white men who had drifted to the edge of civilization and lived in tents or hollowed-out hills. Their beards and hats were covered with dust. They looked tough enough to dig all day or fight one another for an ounce of gold—men of Battling Nelson's stripe. And yet they cheered Gans, jostling to get a look at the newest visitor. They had read, or heard, that he was the consummate boxer—that he could jab and feint and block punches like no other, that he possessed knockout power in both fists and that his hardest punches traveled only inches, that he would patiently wait for his opening and then take it, that he was a virtuoso. They understood him to be a gentleman in the ring who observed rules that others such as Nelson routinely ignored. By their imaginings alone, they seemed to like him and his understated qualities, and they were ready to root for him. To be sure, many referred to him as "a good nigger," a man of calm demeanor who acted the way they thought a black man should, humbly and politely. But they also appreciated the fact that he was the first of the two fighters to arrive, that in effect he was bringing a championship fight, perhaps a historic one, to their unforgiving outpost—a place, one man wrote, "where the desolations meet."

Their excitement was enough to suggest that at least some appreciated him unconditionally for his talent and his decency—there was always plenty of decency and fairness in America—maybe because he had come clean about his past, maybe because they could sense that he was not so different from them. They were all underdogs. *The Goldfield Daily Sun* reported that "if there is race prejudice in Goldfield it was overcome by this plucky lightweight." According to the newspaper, Gans arrived "like a conquering hero or a governor just before election."

The reception took him by surprise.

A man named Larry Sullivan introduced himself as president of the Goldfield Athletic Club and president of the L. M. Sullivan Trust Company. Sullivan had a car, a sure sign of success—a new open-air job with the steering wheel on the right. Off to town they went, about a mile. Along the way, Sullivan revealed his angle. He wanted to be the fighter's manager, and he had whatever money Gans would require.

Sullivan had operated a sailors' rooming house in Seattle where drunken patrons often awakened from their stupors to find themselves at sea, having been kidnapped to work on ships bound for the Orient. Lawrence M. Sullivan was notorious on the West Coast as "Shanghai Larry."

Boomtowns such as Goldfield attracted his like.

At his office, Sullivan offered to pay the $5,000 Gans needed to post as a guarantee that he would show up to fight. Gans didn't have $5,000, so he had no choice but to accept.

"If you lose, you'll never get out of Goldfield alive," Sullivan told him. "My friends are going to bet a ton of money on you. They will kill you if you don't beat Nelson."

Gans took the threat with a laugh.

"If I had any money," he replied calmly, "I'd bet it on myself."

3

When Tex Rickard died from a gangrenous appendix in 1929, New Yorkers by the thousands lined the streets and craned from fire escapes and rooftops to give him a send-off reminiscent, at least to one writer, of that accorded Rudolph Valentino a few years earlier. Rickard was the man who gave them Jack Dempsey, produced the first million-dollar fight, promoted the two Dempsey–Gene Tunney title fights, and headed a group that built the Madison Square Garden on Eighth Avenue between Forty-ninth and Fiftieth Street. He made New York City the boxing capital of the world, an appellation that outlived him by decades. To help keep the Garden thriving, he even founded a professional hockey team; New York's Rangers took their nickname from Rickard's Texas roots.

In 1906, George Lewis Rickard was a saloon owner in Goldfield, and highly successful at the expense of the miners. He had honed his skill in several boomtowns in the Yukon and Alaska during the gold rush of the late nineteenth century. On many occasions, he increased business in those establishments by bringing together two willing brutes, making room in the center of the floor, and letting them beat each other up with their bare fists. One winter, he put on a few fights in a theater in Nome, close enough to the Arctic Circle that Goldfield seemed cosmopolitan by comparison. He knew the sport in its rawest form, but business was such in Goldfield that he never needed crude sluggers.

Tex Rickard contradicted the already established behavioral

stereotype of the promoter as a flamboyant character. Rickard had the demeanor of an office clerk, a quiet man, always well dressed, who looked as if he might be happy adding columns of figures all day and heading home at 5:00 p.m. In reality, he was restless, and with a taste for adventure he spent much of his life on the move. He was born in 1871 in a cabin in western Missouri, near the Kansas border. He was only four years old when he reached his first frontier; his father, seeking a healthier climate, traveled south by covered wagon and relocated in Texas. At age eleven, Rickard joined a cattle drive and rode north with cowboys. For several autumns, he repeated the experience and thrilled to it each time. Eventually, he tried to do what his parents had expected of him and settled down in Henrietta, Texas. In 1894, he married a doctor's daughter and became city marshal. He arranged social events such as picnics, barbecues, and dances, an early sign of his promotional skills. But there was another side to him—he would sneak away to play cards for money and drink whiskey. In 1895, his infant son died, and a month later, so did his brokenhearted wife, who had never recovered from childbirth. In despair, he packed up and shipped north about as far as he could go. While he was on a steamer out of Seattle, a man wanting to buy him a drink called out, "Come on, Tex," and the nickname stuck.

In Alaska, he preferred to make his money off the gold diggers rather than soil his white collar to dig for gold himself. He owned the most famous bar and gambling parlor in all the territory, which luckily he opened just before gold was discovered nearby. He named his place, appropriately, the Northern.

Prospectors on their return to California told of the gold to be found, and of the huge crowds at Rickard's saloon where no cheating was allowed at the gaming tables. For the better part of a decade, Rickard parlayed the role of genial host and discreet cardsharp into half a million dollars, only to gamble away all but about $65,000. After seven years in the north, he came back to the states, remarried, and planned to buy a ranch like the one he had grown up on. Instead, he heard of another gold strike, this one in Nevada, and the possibilities appealed to him, so he rushed to Goldfield. In February 1905, he opened another Northern. At its peak, Goldfield had fifty-three saloons, but the Northern was always the most popular. It boasted fourteen gaming tables and a sixty-foot mahogany bar manned twenty-four hours a day by three shifts of workers. The lawman Wyatt Earp, a gambler himself, worked there for a time as a pit boss.

Rickard also served as Goldfield's unofficial banker. He held miners' money for safekeeping in a back room of the Northern, and he made loans to those he believed had a good chance of striking gold. He was part owner of the Ely, Nevada, Copper Company and a director of the White Pine County Bank.

He belonged to a group of Goldfield businessmen who met to discuss ways of publicizing the town to attract investors from around the country to its mining stocks. In July 1906, he casually mentioned the possibility of a prizefight, noting that all these years after James J. Corbett beat John L. Sullivan for the heavyweight title in 1892, people still talked about it. His colleagues agreed that boxing had its appeal and could attract attention to Goldfield, and on the spot they formed the Goldfield Athletic Club and put him in charge of arranging a prizefight. They realized he knew little about boxing, but he was polite and made a good impression with his low-key manner and impeccable attire. Tall and trim, he dressed in three-piece suits with starched shirts, ties, and collar pins. He usually wore a light-colored fedora, carried a gold-headed Malacca cane, and smoked a cigar. His eyes were ice blue and narrow. A smile often played at his thin lips, giving him an air of confidence; some said he perfected the look while conning other card players into thinking he held the winning hand.

He thought of a few boxers whose names were familiar to him. One was the former featherweight champion Terry McGovern, from Brooklyn. Having no idea that by 1906 McGovern was past his prime, Rickard wired one of the fighter's comanagers, Joe Humphreys, in New York: CAN MAKE YOU AN OFFER OF FIF-TEEN THOUSAND DOLLARS FOR A FIGHT TO THE FINISH BE-TWEEN TERRY MCGOVERN AND JIMMY BRITT TO TAKE PLACE AT GOLDFIELD NEVADA.

Humphreys had never heard of Rickard or Goldfield. Be-sides, he thought, nobody guaranteed money like that. Whoever Rickard was, Humphreys decided he was crazy and fired off a return wire declining the proposal.

Meanwhile, friends enlightened Rickard that since Jim Jef-fries's retirement as heavyweight champion, Gans-Nelson might make a memorable match. Inside the ropes, Gans was an artist, Nelson a wild man who was impervious to pain and virtually im-possible to knock out. Sportswriters had been calling for a meet-ing of the two. "Rickard thought he could sell their meeting as a struggle for racial superiority, not just a boxing match," Geoffrey C. Ward wrote in *Unforgivable Blackness: The Rise and Fall of Jack Johnson*. Locating Gans in San Francisco, Rickard invited him to come to Goldfield immediately. By happenstance, Nelson had been expressing an interest in fighting in Goldfield because a decent lightweight named Jack Clifford was there and chal-lenging all comers. Nelson was reasonably close by, appearing as an added attraction in a vaudeville show in Salt Lake City. Each day, he would go a few easy rounds with some of the locals. He carried a minister named Willard Bean, "the Mormon Pugilist," for three rounds.

Nelson sent a telegram to *The Goldfield Daily Sun* saying that he would take on Clifford for $5,000 plus a guarantee that he could make a $5,000 side bet.

Rickard stepped in with the reply: YOUR PROPOSITION OF

$5,000 GUARANTEE AND $5,000 SIDE BET ACCEPTED, BUT WOULD PREFER A MEETING BETWEEN YOURSELF AND GANS. WE WILL GIVE $15,000 FOR SAME.

With such an enticement, Nelson's hard-bargaining manager, Billy Nolan, wired Rickard: THIRTY THOUSAND DOLLARS FOR FINISH FIGHT BETWEEN NELSON AND GANS. POST CASH.

YOUR PROPOSITION IS ACCEPTED, Rickard answered hastily. He thought Nolan was about to have Nelson sign with another promoter in a different place. And Nolan took the bait of $30,000—by far the largest guaranteed purse ever. By accident, Rickard was on the verge of arranging what promised to be a bigger fight than even the heavyweight battles of the 1890s in which the title changed hands: Corbett over Sullivan, Bob Fitzsimmons over Corbett, Jeffries over Fitzsimmons. And by accident, Rickard came to realize that offering the fighters huge sums of money would help create excitement, a scheme he would use many times in the future.

Rickard acted quickly to cover the $30,000, boasting later that within an hour he had enticed Goldfield's eager businessmen to put up more than enough: $52,000. George Graham Rice, a pseudonym for Jacob Simon Herzig, a twice-convicted swindler from the East Coast who would become more notorious as "the Jackal of Wall Street," promised to do his part. More significantly, Rickard had the support of George Wingfield, well on his way to becoming the most powerful man in Nevada in 1906 when he and Senator George Nixon in a multimillion-dollar deal combined six of Goldfield's mining claims into the Goldfield Consolidated Mines Company with financial help from, among others, Bernard Baruch and Henry Clay Frick.

Rickard went to the John S. Cook & Co. Bank, next door to the Northern, and arranged to have the $30,000 exhibited in stacks of twenty-dollar gold pieces. The idea suggested Rickard's promotional genius. Newspapers across the country published photographs of the fifteen hundred neatly stacked coins. Sports editors planned to dispatch their best reporters to Goldfield to cover the fight.

Next, Rickard trekked to Reno to court Billy Nolan, having learned that Nolan could be troublesome before contracts were signed. Rickard could charm. He persuaded Nolan to accept two-thirds of the purse: Rickard told him that the fight publicity would be extraordinary, his man would surely win, and even bigger money awaited in future fights. Nolan was satisfied to accept, on behalf of Nelson, more money than any participant in a prize-fight had ever received.

4

In addition to the money, $22,500 of what grew to be a $33,500 purse, Rickard agreed to every outrageous demand Nolan made. The most unreasonable was Nolan's stipulation about the weigh-in, which was written into the agreement signed by the fighters on August 12. While ordinarily a fighter weighs in only once, Gans would have to weigh in at noon, one-thirty, and three o'clock, only minutes before fight time, to ensure that he was at or below 133 pounds, then the lightweight limit.

Nelson would weigh in three times as well, but his doing so would be a formality; he never had trouble making weight. With age, however, Gans had found it increasingly difficult to weigh in at 133. Over the years, he had grown into a welterweight, but he continued to take off weight because there was more money to be made as a lightweight. However, he had never been required to adhere to such an absurd proposition as three weigh-ins. The last weigh-in, just minutes before the opening bell, would leave him no time to replenish his body with liquids. Nolan intended for the restrictions to weaken Gans's strength and power.

Days later, Nolan said that Gans would have to weigh in each time wearing his fighting gear, which meant his trunks, shoes, and gloves. Taking the extra items into account, he would have to weigh about 130 ¾, 2 ¼ pounds below the limit. If he was over-weight at noon, Nolan said he would claim Gans's forfeit money of $5,000 and require Gans to post another $5,000 for the second weigh-in, and if overweight again, another $5,000. Since Gans didn't have the money, Larry Sullivan would have to cover any additional costs. "I'll weigh in harness. I will agree to anything to have the fight come off," Gans said.

Nolan had another requirement. He wanted as small a ring as possible, eighteen feet on a side, giving Gans less room to dance and avoid Nelson's predictable roughhousing. "I could fight on top of a Saratoga trunk if I had to," Gans said.

The Salt Lake Herald scolded Nolan for his "dictatorial tactics."

The Denver Post did so as well: "Nolan claimed everything but the earth for his fighter . . ."

A *Denver Times* article denounced Nolan and praised Gans—in the vernacular of newspapers written for white audiences. "The bold bandit, Butch Cassidy, has been run to earth at last," the paper said. "Under the alias of Bill Nolan . . . he was discovered in Goldfield yesterday, holding up a coon."

The Goldfield Daily Sun predicted that the fight would not take place were it not for Gans's concessions. *The Goldfield News*, a serious weekly devoted almost exclusively to mining camp coverage, reported that Gans's willingness to submit to Nolan's impositions "won the hearts of Goldfielders," and more: "Gans is the favorite and the camp finds itself in the unique position of wishing to see a negro defeat a white man."

In two cartoons, one published before he reached Goldfield and the other after his arrival, the *Tonopah Daily Sun* changed its depiction of Gans from an absurd racist caricature to a well-dressed, stately figure.

Rickard, for his part, had no interest in making things fair for a black boxer, although it cost him nothing to praise the man he sought to swindle by stating the obvious: "I must say Gans has acted the fairest way in the world . . . by giving way to the demands of Nolan as well as acquiescing in anything asked for . . . Gans has made many friends by his actions." It was never likely that Nolan would cancel the fight if his demands weren't met, but Rickard might have had to increase Nelson's purse to keep his promotion intact and, not incidentally, turn a profit himself.

With Gans and Nelson, Rickard could begin his promotional tour de force by playing the race card. There had been mixed-race bouts, but irregularly, and there had never been one of this caliber. Gans versus Nelson loomed as the most profitable fight ever.

Ed Moriarty, of the *Los Angeles Herald*, called it "the greatest contest scheduled within the memory of ring followers."

The *Chicago Daily Tribune* sports editor and columnist George Siler wrote: "The conditions imposed by Nolan, the size of the purse, the unlimited distance set for the battle, and the reputation of the men make it the most important contest of the century."

"The Battle of the Century," *The Goldfield Daily Sun* proclaimed. Just that summer, Harry K. Thaw had committed "the Crime of the Century" when he shot Stanford White, the former lover of Evelyn Nesbit, Thaw's wife, on the roof of the building he had designed, New York's second Madison Square Garden.

Teddy Roosevelt, who sparred in the White House basement, found time while turning America into a world power to follow news of the forthcoming "Battle of the Century" in Goldfield.

Gans wired a message to a friend. He said to come on from San Francisco and bring his trunk.

5

Even though he was the champion, Gans had come to expect unfair treatment. Blacks ranked at the bottom of society—sports society, too. Many whites considered blacks a kind of subspecies. In Gans's time, separate but equal had become the law and American apartheid the reality.

As America's new capitalists amassed fortunes and built monuments to themselves, a great gulf was growing between them and the poor. Wealth was cornered by a small percentage of the population, and opportunity depended above all else on one's skin color. Blacks' life expectancy was roughly a third shorter than whites'. *Plessy v. Ferguson* upheld racial segregation under the guise of separate but equal, when the reality was separate and unequal.

Waiting for a trolley one day in Baltimore, Gans was approached by a police officer, a big man, who growled, "Nigger, what are you doing sitting there?"

"I was just sitting here waiting for the streetcar," Gans said.

"Get up, nigger. Stand up when you talk to me."

When Gans stood up, the officer struck him with his club. The blow landed on Gans's arm. The cop intended to hit him again when a sergeant who had been watching rushed up.

"What's going on here?"

"Why, this nigger got smart with me, and I'm going to teach him a lesson."

"Wait a minute," the sergeant commanded. "This man is a gentleman. Don't you know that's Joe Gans, the lightweight champion of the world?"

Plenty of whites, had they known about the incident, would have wished that the racist cop had clubbed Gans into submission. Some of his victories over white opponents set off fights between blacks and whites in Baltimore's streets and in other cities. People had begun to take boxing seriously, even though it was illegal in most places. Its appeal was in its simplicity, and its violence, and the glamorous figures it produced.

"Everybody knew Joe Gans," an elderly Baltimore woman, a child in his times, said. "He was in the papers."

Many of the stories attempted to explain away his success. He was depicted as a "thinking" fighter, which he was, but the characterization was meant to make him seem as white as could be. "Black—yes—but white to the core," one newspaper article described him. Another quoted an acquaintance of Gans as saying, "Joe, you're the whitest nigger I ever seen." The *New York American* splashed a story on its first sports page suggesting that he was Egyptian.

In 1902, Gans knocked out Frank Erne with a single punch in one minute and forty seconds to become the lightweight champion. He was in his prime, in the midst of an unbeaten streak of forty-two fights. But as often happens in the life of a boxer, the most promising possibilities occur late, sometimes even in the twilight of brilliance. So it was for Gans—almost coincident with his court testimony that he was on boxing's downward slope. In 1905, Jim Jeffries's unexpected retirement as heavyweight champion left no obvious successor. An up-and-coming black fighter named Jack Johnson might have taken charge, but he lost a decision to a white fighter in San Francisco that even avowed racists acknowledged was a travesty. Johnson's ascent was interrupted, and many boxing fans turned to other weight classes for their entertainment. And there was Gans, and there was the similarly famous Nelson, with reputations unsurpassed. Gans was the champion; Nelson, with flawed reasoning, claimed to be. A meeting of the two was a matchup unlike any the sport had yet confected.

6

Goldfield was as bleak as Parmeter Kent in his newspaper had made it out to be. Spare wooden buildings lined dirt streets crowded with people, horse-drawn wagons, and an occasional automobile trying to squeeze by. Every place was packed with humanity: general stores, food stores, a half-dozen banks. Water wagons offered some relief from the blistering sun and the airless shops. It was unrelentingly hot.

Saloons operated on all four corners of Main Street and Crook Avenue. Fortunes could be won or lost in minutes. Rickard's Northern had a roulette wheel inside the door, the dealer standing in shirtsleeves and vest; unshaven miners tossed down ten-dollar gold pieces onto black or red as if they were pennies. Farther along in the narrow, dimly lit room could be found the occasional distinguished-looking card player, attired typically in a gray or black Stetson, black Prince Albert coat, dark trousers stuffed into high boots, white shirt, and black string tie.

"Most of the men wear guns and there has been some gun play," one woman wrote in a letter home. "Jack Longstreet, who I am told has long been a desperado in our part of Nevada and who once lived close to Las Vegas, rides shotgun on the stages between here and Tonopah. He is a fearful looking old man with long hair which is rumored to hide the loss of an ear cut off for horse stealing." Longstreet was tall and had steel blue eyes and five notches on his Colt .44—a midcareer Clint Eastwood.

Goldfield was home to the likes of Kid Foley, a lawbreaker turned deputy sheriff, whose principal job seemed to be repeatedly ejecting "the Dogface Kid," a boisterous nuisance, from the Northern; and the more dangerous Kid Kendall, a miserable teenager not unlike Billy the Kid, whose fate was to be shot dead by an adversary, Doc Sharp.

The risk of instant death was an inconvenience, nothing more. The handful of wooden hotels had few vacancies. So did its tent hotels. A placard above the front flap of one identified it as the Waldorf-Astoria. Sheets were hung as partitions, but the sleepers were bunched together so tightly they often were awakened in the darkness by a snoring neighbor who would roll over and bump them from the other side of the divider.

Miners' tents encircled the downtown. At night, yellow-gray coyotes howled in the moonlight.

There was a red-light district: a row of tiny houses, each scarcely spacious enough for a bed, each with a bay window and a nameplate affixed alongside: Sadie, Sylvia, Jessie . . . Between customers, the occupant sat in front of her window as an in-the-flesh advertisement.

There were opium dens, which also offered cocaine and morphine and produced almost four hundred addicts; several dance halls; and a place called "the Bank," which actually was one of the many saloons.

Sullivan chauffeured Gans around town and to its outskirts, passing among the mines and bragging how hundreds of thousands of dollars' worth of gold were being excavated each day. "You have so much wealth up here," Gans said, "you ought to give us a $500,000 purse, and the preliminary fighters a $30,000 purse."

For those who could afford to eat out, there were at least two decent restaurants, Ajax's Parisienne, owned by a Victor Ajax and located amid the brothels, and the Palm Grill, which featured quail on toast and served its dinners on fine china set on thick linen as Julius Goldsmith played the violin.

Rickard lived in one of the few substantial homes. It was made of brick and had a small, lush lawn surrounded by a white picket fence. The house had indoor plumbing, electric lights, and stained-glass windows. Rickard drove a Thomas Flyer, which could go sixty miles an hour with its sixty-horsepower engine. Someone said of Rickard that "luck gave him the cards and he knew how to play them."

7

Rickard arranged for Gans to live and train at the Merchants Hotel, next to Columbia Mountain, about a mile north of the center of town. The place was quiet and surprisingly comfortable. Gans was presented with a three-room suite. At seven o'clock each morning, he ran as much as nine miles back and forth on a dirt road. After that, he took a bath, had a rubdown and a rest, and ate lunch. Early each afternoon, he greeted admirers and posed for photographs. Usually, he wore khaki trousers and a jersey and sat in an easy chair. At three-thirty, he worked in a gym that had been hastily built behind the hotel. He punched the light bag, then hammered a forty-pound bag of sawdust. He sparred several rounds. He skipped rope, as many as a thousand times a session. And to get accustomed to the desert's glare, he shadowboxed just outside the gym door in the late afternoon's slanting sun.

"At the Gans camp everything is working like a Seth Thomas clock," *The Goldfield Daily Sun* reported.

Gans played poker at his hotel, without much luck. Casey McDonald, the hotel's proprietor, invited him into a game. Shortly, McDonald showed two pair.

"Not enough," Gans said, showing a straight.

"It's really too bad, Joe, but we don't play straights out in this country."

McDonald took the pot. But, a few minutes later, he split it with Gans.

Visitors found Gans extremely cordial. "He impressed me as a quiet, well-mannered, intelligent colored man, humorous and shrewdly observant," the author Rex Beach once wrote. Those traits contributed to his appeal among whites. Larry Sullivan, for one, had a change of heart about Gans after getting to know him. Sullivan was impressed by Gans's earnestness in training and his easygoing nature. Instead of trying to take advantage of him, as he had intended to do, Sullivan served him well while he was in Goldfield. Sullivan hired a secretary to handle all the telegrams and letters sent to Gans. One day, Sullivan even tried to keep up with Gans during a training run by riding a horse, but the horse threw the 200-pounder and shook him up, landing him in bed for a day.

Nevada governor John Sparks, drawn to Gans as politicians and entertainers have always gravitated to celebrated athletes, showed up to introduce himself.

"Well, you're going to see the fight of your life," Gans promised him.

"I will pardon the man that lives," Sparks said grandly. Gans feigned fright.

"Governor, I don't want to kill no man."

The "happiest man in camp"—that's how a reporter described Gans. One day in front of his hotel, he made a joke of all the talk in town that he was having trouble making the 133-pound weight limit: He posed for a goofy photograph in which a sparring partner, Charlie Simms, held his leg outstretched and trainer Frank McDonald pretended to saw it off so that he could make weight.

Having dinner with those helping him train and enjoying the sounds of the piano in the hotel lobby were nightly pleasures. He stamped the floor, keeping time with the music. One evening, he delighted guests by singing a medley of ragtime tunes.

8

Visitors to Gans's camp could not help but notice the presence of a beautiful woman. "His handsome mulatto wife," one reporter called her. And at ringside, where she had watched Joe's fights, she could be even more eye-catching. On one occasion, seated behind the press bench, she wore a long-coated suit of cream-colored tennis flannel and a white felt picture hat decorated with a green plume, set off by a dotted mesh veil.

Sometimes she watched him prepare for Nelson in the afternoons at their hotel's gym, which seated about 200. Spectators tried to analyze her reactions to what was happening in the ring, but training is repetitious and boring, and so she merely looked as serious as he did, preparing for the fight of his life. He usually wore black tights and worked up a sweat, but appeared to have plenty of energy.

During an afternoon off from training, she and Gans were taken on a leisurely drive to neighboring Tonopah in Larry Sullivan's automobile. Many evenings she would play the piano in the hotel lobby. "Mrs. Gans, who is exceptionally well educated, surprised everybody by her ability as a musician," a newspaper reported. Gans introduced her all around, and the press referred to her, without exception and without mention of a first name, as "Mrs. Gans."

Except she wasn't. Not yet, anyway. She was Martha Davis, a teacher from Baltimore who graduated from the Colored High

School in 1900. But in Goldfield, she was a single woman keeping company with Gans, who was very much married to Madge Wadkins. In July 1905, he had filed for divorce. Madge countered by suing Martha Davis "for the alienation of her husband's affections," charging that Davis "wrongfully caused" him to abandon her. As part of her testimony, she promised to produce "some compromising letters from Martha Davis" to her husband.

The judge's recommendation that Madge and Joe try to reconcile proved to be fanciful thinking. Martha Davis traveled with Gans to several West Coast bouts. And she would be with him at ringside in Goldfield.

In fact, Gans had been married three times. His first wife was Florence Reed. Both she and Gans were about nineteen years old when they married on September 17, 1893, in Baltimore. He gave his name as "Joseph Gant." The marriage ended in divorce after the birth of a son, James, whose death certificate names Joseph Gans and Florence Reed as his parents. The death certificate of Julia Gans, which names Joseph Gans and Florence as her parents, lists only 1890 as her date of birth. On May 21, 1895, Gans, again giving his name as "Joseph Gant" and again describing himself as "single," married another local woman, Mary Beulah Spriggs. Within months, however, she was diagnosed with consumption, later known as tuberculosis. Summoned back to Baltimore from New York, where he was preparing for a fight, Gans took up a bedside vigil in their home at 1426 East Lexington Street. She died a few days later, on March 18, 1896.

At the time, tuberculosis was rampant in crowded cities, and Baltimore was one of the most densely populated places in the country. There was little to combat the disease, which causes difficulty in breathing. The infection could lie dormant in the body and allow a person to continue normal living, or it could flare up and kill you. Tuberculosis killed more than a million Americans in the first decade of the twentieth century. It killed blacks, it killed whites, it killed the young. TB was the great scourge.

Within a year of Mary Beulah's death, Gans fathered a daughter out of wedlock. She grew up with a family in East Baltimore, and Gans is said to have provided money to the woman who raised the child. The daughter was able to keep her father's name. She was Gertrude Gans. "My father always said that Joe Gans was his grandfather," Arlene Maxwell of Baltimore said of her late father, Slater Brown, Jr., "and he was very proud of it."

9

Growing up in Baltimore, Joe Gans found himself having to engage in a "battle royal"—a melee of black boys in the ring that
white theater customers found uproarious. It was the same predicament faced by the protagonist in Ralph Ellison's *Invisible Man*.

> Blindfolded, I could no longer control my motions. I had
> no dignity. I stumbled about like a baby or a drunken man.
> The smoke had become thicker and with each new blow it
> seemed to sear and further restrict my lungs. My saliva be-
> came like hot bitter glue. A glove connected with my head,
> filling my mouth with warm blood. It was everywhere . . . I
> felt myself going over, my head hitting the floor. Streaks of
> blue light filled the black world behind the blindfold. I lay
> prone, pretending that I was knocked out, but felt myself
> seized by hands and yanked to my feet. "Get going, black
> boy! Mix it up!"

Gans did not have to wear a blindfold, but Baltimore had
its own variations, one of which H. L. Mencken described as
"the device of dressing the colored boys who fought in battles
royal, not in ordinary trunks, but in the billowy white drawers
that women then wore. The blacker the boy, the more striking
the effect."

Whatever Gans's precise experience, he did not come out of it bitter for a couple of reasons. He was bent on becoming a prize-fighter and believed that the battle royal was the only way to begin. He also had a mother who loved him. Actually, she was his foster mother who raised him from his early years, teaching him a graciousness that she thought would help him cope with the unfairness and cruelties he would face growing up black. From her he gained a considerable facility with the language, and a sense of humor.

Gans's birth date is generally given as November 25, 1874, but his death certificate has it as September 1, 1874, and Gans himself said he didn't know what the date was. He was named after his father, Joseph Butts. Little is known about Butts except that he played baseball for black teams on the Baltimore sand-lots. The boy's mother is unknown. Butts had no interest in rais-ing a child, but he knew a couple who did. James Gant, a fish market worker, and his wife, Maria, adopted the boy when he was four. He became Joseph Gant—"Gans" would come later from a newspaper misspelling after a reporter at one of his early fights got the name wrong.

The Gants lived in a brick row house at 334 Eastern Avenue, not far from the waterfront. Maria Gant enrolled Joe in Primary School No. 2 at 200 East Street, near Lexington Street, but how long he stayed is uncertain. James Gant got him a job as an er-rand boy. Later, he worked at a stall in one of the sheds of Centre Market, popularly known as Marsh Market, because it stood on what had been marshland adjacent to Jones Falls, close to the harbor. The Chesapeake Bay teemed with crabs and oysters, clams and shrimp, and fish of all kinds, and they were brought up the Patapsco River to Baltimore and taken from the boats in overloaded trays and piled high on ice in the stalls. People would crowd around in anarchy, making their picks from the daily haul. In decent weather, people would drink coffee and talk.

Working there, however, offered few pleasures. Gans cleaned fish. And he shucked oysters, one at a time, separating the shells with a knife, then freeing the oyster by cutting the muscle that held it to the shell. It was a tedious job but one that could be done expeditiously with practice. He worked long hours. He had to report before sunup, to help unload the boats and farm wagons, and he stayed all day. In winter, the market's dirt floors turned to a bone-chilling mud. Winds blew beneath the eaves. Workers warmed themselves with small fires in buckets behind the counters.

In a nearby dirt square, horse-drawn wagons and carts were parked at hitching posts in front of buildings where tobacco and whiskey were housed and sold—boys who worked in the market shot dice or engaged in fistfights. Gans liked to shoot dice. He had no desire to fight. But he encountered a boy's usual challenges. Once, he beat an older and bigger boy into a bloody mess, but not before demonstrating a keen entrepreneurial bent: He persuaded his antagonist to hold off until a crowd gathered and a hat could be passed.

Caleb Bond, the fishmonger for whom Gans worked, recognized the boy's intelligence and was impressed by his fighting ability. Bond, by chance, was an amateur boxing coach. He bought Gans a pair of boxing gloves and interested him in the science of the sport, molding his student into a calculating boxer. As part of his training regimen, Bond had the prospect box two boys at once to develop defensive skills, to learn to avoid punches from different directions. Bond taught him to move his head and block with his gloves and forearms, and to waste little motion so he could save his energy and punch crisply. Bond believed in body punching and in patience, waiting for the opening and counterpunching. Following instructions, Gans would glide toward an opponent behind a stiff left jab. He learned to put together combinations of punches. And he developed short, straight blows instead of the roundhouse swings favored by most fighters of the era.

One night after work, Gans walked a block east on Baltimore

Street and presented himself to James L. Kernan, who owned and managed the yellow-brick Monumental Theatre, the city's premier vaudeville house. It was a big building with a stage curtain that carried advertisements for Riverview Park, Dr. Becker's Medical Museum, Swerdloe's dress suits, and the largest beer in the city for five cents. Kernan carried a long stick, and before the curtain went up, he would rap the stick on the back of a seat and shout: "Hats off, everybody. Silence." Years later, a hospital would bear his name as the result of his philanthropy, and he would own a hotel where Al Jolson stayed and Fred Astaire and Ginger Rogers danced in its Marble Bar. But in 1890 Kernan was seeking ways to fill the seats for the traveling shows he had booked. Hoping to attract crowds, he had his pit musicians play outside on the sidewalk before performances. He put on boxing matches before the stage shows and would open the bouts with a battle royal. Kernan, at least, cautioned the sixteen-year-old Gans.

"You probably don't realize what a rough game this is," he said. "You've got to go right in and slug and keep swinging as long as another competitor is still on his feet. If you quit, you don't get a cent."

Gans won his first battle royal, and then a second. Maria Gant was surprised to find him carrying so much money—Kernan paid $5 for each victory. Initially, Gans kept from her the fact that he was boxing, although she was anxious to know whether he was making the money honestly. One day, by his account, another adult who lived with the family—Gans referred to him as his "uncle," a boarder named William Pennington—asked where the money was coming from. Gans invited the man to join him that evening to watch the fights at the Monumental. At the box office, Gans asked for and received two free tickets. As he and his "uncle" were walking down the aisle to their seats in the front row, a white man in the audience excitedly pointed out young Joe's arrival. The "uncle" was mystified by it all. After a while,

Gans told him to stay seated, and he disappeared. Shortly, he climbed into the ring. "You never saw a man look as queer as he did when I appeared on the stage," Gans said. "I put my opponent out, but I could hardly do it for looking at my uncle."

With that, he confessed to his foster mother: He made his windfall fighting at the Monumental. He proposed quitting the fish market to become a full-time prizefighter. She had hoped he would earn his livelihood in one of the markets, where, she thought, he could find dignity and his way against the hard current of bigotry. Reluctantly, she let him try his way.

10

Shortly after seeing Gans fight, Al Herford got into the business, ostensibly as a manager. A persuasive talker, Herford had no trouble signing up the young fighter despite an unusually cautionary remark: "I don't know enough as yet, and you might lose your money." To which Herford replied: "I'm satisfied to take a chance."

Herford worked as a bookmaker at the Pimlico racetrack in northwest Baltimore before pari-mutuel betting, and he owned a restaurant on Fleet Street, on the east side of the city, that he had inherited from his father. Herford had his name carved in the sidewalk out front. Power brokers and politicians, sports figures and newspapermen gathered there, allowing Herford to puff his chest against his buttoned vest. Timothy D. Sullivan—"Big Tim," not only big in stature but also a Tammany Hall boss who controlled most of the gambling houses in Manhattan—paid a visit.

Gans was a teenager then, living only blocks from Herford's place but trying to fight his way out of the neighborhood. It wasn't easy. Underprivileged boys already had begun taking up boxing in hopes of earning a living. "It is a solid fact that the sparring profession, like law, labor and medicine, is overcrowded," the Baltimore *Sun* reported in 1890. "It is safe to say that there are in the United States alone ten thousand boxers . . . The number is doubtless increased by a societary trouble that is responsible for other evils, namely, lack of employment."

But many boxers quit the ring in a hurry—it has always been

this way. So if the numbers engaged in prizefighting remained fairly constant, the faces were ever changing. Even some of the more skilled would come to realize after being hit in the head or the body that prizefighting was not the obvious career path it had seemed.

An older man named Kehoe, a furniture mover, beat Gans badly in a trolley car barn at the corner of Pratt Street and Central Avenue in East Baltimore. A less determined young man might have retreated to the safety of cleaning fish. But Gans wanted to learn how he could improve his boxing. And he had Caleb Bond to turn to, and that helped.

An eyewitness gave this account of Gans boxing a journeyman in a house in which the ring was rigged in the shape of a rectangle so it could fit into adjoining parlors: "The 'trial horse' had a trifle the better of the battle and got the decision, but no one who saw the sinewy negro youngster fight that night doubted that he was going to [be] a first-class [boxer]. And it is probably equally true that no one who witnessed that practically first public appearance of Gans dreamed that he would ever attain the pinnacle of fame he was destined to reach."

In one of his early bouts, a white Baltimore boxer named Fred Sweigart declared that the only way Gans could win was by knockout; otherwise Sweigart would get the entire purse and the fight would be ruled a draw. Gans tried for ten rounds to knock out Sweigart, but the veteran survived and took home all the money.

"Kill the nigger," white audiences shouted during Gans's early fights. But as Gans continued, he won over whites with his businesslike manner and effectiveness. In subsequent bouts, white fans shouted for the black man's detractors to be quiet.

One night, Gans took on five different opponents. At least twice, he fought three different men on the same day.

On November 27, 1893, the Avon Club, located in a modest

house on the northwest corner of East Baltimore Street and Central Avenue, held a night of entertainment that included prizefighting. In the last bout on the card, Gans, known then as Joseph Gant, exhibited a ring generalship that the members could not help admiring. In victory, he contrasted noticeably with his opponent, a youngster named William Jones, who mindlessly refused to stop fighting at the end of their six-rounder.

On March 4, 1895, in the Monumental's back room, where stage equipment and extra furniture was stored, Gans—by now, his name had been misspelled in the newspaper, and the new name had stuck—boxed so skillfully that Max Wirsing quit after three rounds. Despite his color, Gans quickly became a top attraction, and almost as quickly, the *Baltimore American* hailed him as "one of the greatest fighters of his class in the country."

Under Herford's orders, Gans was allowed to defeat whites but not too easily, so he often pulled his punches and carried them extra rounds. "In an era of Jim Crow and the Ku Klux Klan . . . an aggressive black fighter who flattened white opponents quickly wouldn't enjoy a profitable or long career—or even a long life," the author Ned Beaumont has written.

On a night he was carrying a white opponent at Al Herford's behest, Gans played a prank on one of his corner men, his friend Kid North. In his day job, North handled bets for one of Baltimore's big-time bookmakers, but sometimes he would book the bets himself, risky business since he usually didn't have the money to cover any losses. For this fight, he booked the anti-Gans money himself. And to his shock as the fight progressed, the opponent scored a lucky punch and dropped Gans momentarily.

Between rounds, North said to Gans: "What's the matter? What did you let him knock you down for, Joe?"

"'Cause he's got two fists," Gans replied, sensing North's desperation. "If you think you can do better, you go out there and fight him the next round."

"Come on, Joe," North said, "you can take him next round."

"I don't know, Kid, I don't know," Gans said.

"My God, man, don't talk like that," North said. "You're the great Joe Gans. You've got to whip him. If you don't, the Kid has got to leave Baltimore or get killed."

Gans toyed with his foe for another round, causing Kid North more distress, before winning by a knockout.

Once, Herford ran a boxing show at the Bijou Opera House in Paterson, New Jersey, that attracted few customers. When the Bijou's proprietor realized there would be no profit, Herford calmed him by giving him the ring off his hand. The next day, when the man discovered he possessed not a diamond but a hunk of glass, Herford was long gone.

As Gans's manager, Herford should have devoted himself to developing his fighter's career, bringing him along slowly and carefully, arranging bouts that he would most likely win but that would teach him something he could then use against tougher opponents. But Herford, always more intent on making money, scheduled matches for Gans that would produce headlines and draw big crowds.

More promoter than manager, Herford matched Gans against the Australian legend known as Young Griffo, an almost unhittable featherweight. Out of the ring, he challenged people to land a blow against him as he stood on a handkerchief. He dodged their punches and blocked others. On fight nights, he often carried a bottle of whiskey into the ring and took swigs between rounds. Gans-Griffo attracted an overflow crowd of three thousand people to Baltimore's Front Street Theatre. They left disappointed. Herford was to blame.

Beforehand, he had told Griffo to go easy on Gans or Gans wouldn't fight. And not wanting to spoil Griffo's reputation by having him knocked out, he had ordered Gans to take it easy, too. "Not a blow in the ten rounds was landed hard enough to break a pane of glass," *The Sun* reported.

Over a decade, Herford took at least half of about $100,000

due Gans from his ring earnings and bets. Gans squandered his half, mostly by gambling. Only once did he try to change managers. In 1896, *The National Police Gazette*—a weekly devoted to vaudeville, boxing, and heinous acts below such headlines as BATTLE WITH CORPSE-EATING CATS and WHIPPING A WIFE-BEATER—reported that Herford paid Gans only $48 for beating Jerry Marshall in a twenty-rounder. Herford gave Marshall $14. So Gans set out on his own, but Herford sought an injunction restraining Gans from appearing under any other manager, asserting that his managerial contract lasted for another two years. A Baltimore court ruled for Herford.

"Slavery in these days is an unknown thing, yet here is a case in direct opposition to this popular notion," *The National Police Gazette* said. "While they may be together now, still it hardly enhances the public opinion of Herford to cling to his lad like a miser to his gold . . . Holding a man in thralldom by law process has never been popular in fistiana."

Not until 1905 was Gans able to sever his business connection with Herford.

11

On April 18, 1906, a Wednesday, Gans was awakened before daybreak by a fierce rumbling. He had been asleep in a house on Market Street in San Francisco, which he had made his temporary home. He was the lightweight champion of the world, and had been since 1902, when he knocked out Frank Erne. He had defended the title nine times. During one stretch he had won thirty straight fights. In January 1906, he had knocked out Mike Sullivan in San Francisco to win the vacant welterweight championship.

It was 5:12 a.m. when the earthquake struck. From a hotel on Market Street, Enrico Caruso, who had appeared as Don Jose in *Carmen* the previous evening at the Grand Opera House, fled in silk pajamas and a fur coat.

Caruso and Gans rushed into the same street.

"I threw open the window, and I think I let out the grandest notes I ever hit in all my life," Caruso said. "I do not know why I did this. I presume I was too excited to do anything else." As the building shook, a colleague rushed into his seventh-floor room, shouting, "My God, it's an earthquake. Get your things and run." Caruso did, with a prized photograph under his arm, and by showing that photograph, he gained admittance to a park filled with frightened people, and there he rested on a patch of grass. The photo was inscribed "With kindest regards from Theodore Roosevelt."

Gans had come to San Francisco seeking opponents after finally breaking with Herford. In April, a matchmaker and sportswriter named Biddy Bishop suggested to Gans that he meet "Philadelphia Jack" O'Brien, the light heavyweight champion, at 154 pounds. Gans and O'Brien were considered the two cleverest boxers. Bishop negotiated with them over the phone, and the three agreed to meet in San Francisco on the evening of the eighteenth. That day, however, things changed.

"San Francisco is gone," Jack London wrote. "Nothing remains of it but memories."

Before the building in which he slept collapsed, Gans hurriedly got into his clothes. He had a few dollars in his pockets, but he lost the rest of his belongings, including sixty dollars in gold pieces that were buried in the rubble. Gans joined a throng headed along Market Street toward the ferries. A street preacher cried out: "Haven't I told you of all this? Haven't I warned you?"

The ferry building was jammed, and people pushed their way onto the boats; some even jumped from the pier and missed, falling into the water. Two days later, Gans met up with Biddy Bishop in a bread line in Oakland.

A few days after that, Gans took a train back to Baltimore. *The Sun* described him as "not looking robust" but reported him saying that he felt well and he was happy.

In May, Gans joined other boxers in New York to put on exhibition bouts at Madison Square Garden to benefit survivors of the earthquake. Gans, to the delight of about seven thousand fans, went three rounds with a heavyweight named "Jabber" Carey.

Caruso, angered by the natural disaster, vowed never to return to San Francisco, and he never did. Gans did, in July, hoping somehow to find riches amid the ruins. It was then that a copy boy from *The San Francisco Call* found him and told him that someone in Goldfield—a Tex Rickard—was looking for him.

12

As Gans trained for Nelson, some thought that he showed the effects of so many years in the ring. In reality, he was an "old" thirty-one for a boxer—old from having fought so often and from repeating the ordeal of shedding weight so many times to make the lightweight limit. Long before Goldfield, the nationally syndicated *New York Journal* cartoonist and writer "TAD"—Thomas Aloysius Dorgan—had dubbed him "the Old Master."

During his workouts sportswriters talked among themselves about how he might fare against a younger man, especially one as violent as Battling Nelson. They couched their dispatches in wary words.

Edward Clarke, of *The San Francisco Call*, reported: "In my opinion, the Baltimorean looked light, thin and weary-eyed, although he did his punching-bag stunt with his usual cleverness."

R. A. Smyth, also of *The Call*, remarked: "There is a suspicion that the colored champion has not the vigor which marked his work up to two years ago."

Gans's age shows unmistakably in a photograph taken of him in profile eight days before the fight. It ran in *The Salt Lake Herald* under the heading "MISTAH" GANS AND HIS SMILE. The smile of the man in the photo seems forced and wan. With his head shaved, he looks almost skeletal. It is no exaggeration to say that, with his jaw slackened and his side teeth exposed, he has the look of a man whose health is in mortal decline.

But most of the famous fighters of the time—white men—picked Gans to win, probably because he had won so often. The temporarily retired heavyweight champion Jim Jeffries predicted that Gans would "slaughter" Nelson, and Bob Fitzsimmons, Terry McGovern, Willie Fitzgerald, Young Corbett, Jimmy Britt, "Sailor Tom" Sharkey, and Abe Attell—talents all—also favored Gans. "I tell you that after this fight, people will forget Gans is a black man," Young Corbett said.

Fighters, especially older ones and even those battered into retirement by age, tend to go with the more veteran combatant, unlike writers, who sometimes prefer to make a bold prediction or envision an up-and-comer about to flourish. Gans had the experience. He had beaten a host of outstanding fighters, including George Siddons, Dal Hawkins, Kid McPartland, George "Elbows" McFadden, Bobby Dobbs, Dave Holly, Rufe Turner, and Young Griffo. The fearsome Jack Blackburn—his maxim was "Let your fist be the referee," when referees were the sole arbiters—had rarely lost before he lost to Gans.

Many white fans across the country, based on some of the newspaper stories leading up to the fight, preferred Gans to Nelson. It was unusual early in the twentieth century for whites to put their money on a black boxer to beat a white, or to root for a black to beat a white, and it would remain so over the years. The 1938 match between Joe Louis and the German Max Schmeling was the great exception, when the black man represented good and his opponent the evils of Nazism. Whites, of course, could accept Gans because of his subdued personality, unlike that of Jack Johnson, who would come along and, as heavyweight champion, flaunt both his superiority to white men and his irresistibility to white women. Certainly, Gans was a "safe" champion for whites in that he held the lightweight title and not the heavyweight championship, which carried the status of alpha male—too much for most whites to bear in the case of Johnson.

That twist—Goldfield's miners favoring Gans, and a stirring for Gans across much of the country—also owed something to Battling Nelson's reputation for foul tactics, and to his disagreeable manager. Nolan refused to budge from any of the stipulations he placed on Gans, and Rickard did not urge Nolan to change his mind. Whatever Nolan wanted, Nolan got.

The people of Goldfield, observing Gans's reaction to Nolan's conduct, realized that not only could he box, he was articulate and had a sense of humor. One day he said wryly, referring to a type of prison shackle then in use, "I suppose Mr. Nolan will want me to wear an Oregon boot next."

13

You may think I am vicious when I am in the ring with a white man, but you should see me when I am fighting a negro," Battling Nelson said.

He was a racist, and a virulent one, although that hardly made him unusual. He was among the majority of American whites who were poorly educated and felt threatened by the unfamiliar. He took part in mixed-race bouts only because he was "compelled" to, he said. In a stab at autobiography titled *Battling Nelson: His Life, Battles and Career*, he emphasized his enmity toward blacks, exposing his lack of decency. In describing his "first mixup with a 'cullud person,'" he called Feathers Vernon "a pretty tough coon." The term "coon" was widely used, sometimes by blacks themselves as they unwittingly slipped into their white-ordained state in life; but with Nelson, one could almost hear the chortling in his written words. He allowed that Christy Williams, whom Nelson knocked down forty-two times and who knocked him down seven times, gave him "the hardest battle of all the coons . . . This coon had a jaw like the hull of the battleship Ohio"—Nelson's idea of a compliment. He remembered "dancing with glee" as Williams lay knocked out, a show of superiority abhorrent to Gans's principles.

Nelson was known to use an elbow to break an opponent's nose or ram a knee into the other man's groin. His most lethal punch was a short hook to the liver or kidney, fist clenched and knuckles up, delivered with the thumb and forefinger leading instead of the last three fingers, almost a karate chop except that the fingers were not extended. It could shoot a pain all the way to the spine and cause the victim to urinate blood for a week. He called it his left half-scissors hook.

Nelson was a hero to the bigots of the Ku Klux Klan and of such racist elements as the White League and the Red Shirts. Many exulted in Nelson's third-round knockout of Black Griffo with a left half-scissors hook, which, Nelson related in his auto-biography, few could stand up to—and here, he used italics to em-phasize his point—*particularly the negro boxing population.*

He delighted in knocking out another black boxer, Ed Burley, who had to be "carried out of the ring on a wheelbarrow." Nelson wrote: "Oh! It was a shame to do it . . ." But he had to do it quickly, in five rounds, he said, because he was hungry and needed the five dollars badly for "coffee and sinkers."

The longer a fight, the better Nelson liked it. He had the slow heartbeat of a distance runner. His jaw had the resilience of con-crete, and he was always willing to take a punch to give one. Early in his career, one Joe Hedmark floored him seventeen times, but failed to stop him.

"I ain't human," Nelson delighted in saying.

Parts of the medical community agreed. "A blow which would render the usual man unconscious would have no effect on Nel-son," one doctor declared.

Nelson was born Oscar Mattheus Nielsen on Independence Day in Denmark, June 5, 1882. His father called him Battling, explaining that the baby was born battling. The son liked to in-sert the nickname into his formal name, making it Oscar Battling Matthew Nelson. In 1883, the family moved to the United States, settling in Hegewisch, Illinois, which a few years later became part of Chicago's far South Side. Nelson disliked school and dropped out. In winters, he cut blocks of ice from Lake Michigan and helped haul them by horse and wagon to downtown Chicago markets. He worked for a man named John Daline, "the Ice Man of Hegewisch," advancing from fifteen cents a week to a dollar. He also earned a dollar a week working as a meat cutter in a packinghouse. The jobs hardened him into a street tough. In September 1896, Wallace's Circus came to nearby Hammond, Indiana, and Nelson talked his way into carrying water for elephants. That earned him a pass to the show, which included a strongman known as Wallace's Kid, who took on all comers. Of the power in his fists, the circus manager declared: "The very sting of death is in every blow." Nelson, then fourteen, standing little more than five feet tall but with the muscular upper body and broad chest of a boxer, applied to challenge him.

Wallace's Kid and Nelson met in a tent crowded with spectators, gathered, some from great distances, to see things they ordinarily wouldn't. The bell sounded, and Wallace's Kid hurled himself toward the boy. But before the big man could throw a punch, Nelson shot a left uppercut to the middle of the Kid's face, drawing blood from his nose and mouth. The Kid staggered. For the next minute or so, Nelson followed up with a series of blows that would become his trademark style. He landed punches relentlessly against a weakened opponent. Before the first round had ended, the Kid hit the dust, knocked out.

The manager reneged on his promise to pay Nelson one dollar—with the same persistence he would display in the ring, the fighter collected it sixteen years later when, by chance, he met up with the same circus in Lawrence, Kansas—but Nelson decided anyway that he wanted to be a prizefighter. In 1897, he fought for the "championship of Hegewisch" at the local boys' club, and he won in the third round when his opponent cried, "Enough!" That evening, Nelson left a note for his parents and ran away to seek his future in the ring.

In South Dakota, he worked as a meat cutter, a ranch hand,

and a waiter in a hotel restaurant. On consecutive days in May 1898, in Sioux Falls, he beat Freddie Green, a stylish boxer known as "the Champion of the Dakotas," and Soldier Williams, a plodder who had been in the Army. He knocked out both and earned a total of $17.50. As if he had proved a point, Nelson returned home to Hegewisch, and for the next four years he fought in and around Chicago. He won a string of fights, and after each he displayed little humility. A fellow named Eddie Penny fell in one round as a result of "great slugging—on my part—mostly," Nelson boasted in his autobiography. "In fact, Penny hardly touched me with one good punch during the short mix-up, from the call of time up to the point where I reached out and cracked him into unconsciousness."

One day in December 1901, a boxing promoter walked into a pool parlor on Wabash Avenue seeking a substitute for a bout to be held in two hours. Nelson, who was shooting pool, accepted the challenge, even though his opponent would be a middleweight. The poolroom crowd tagged along to the nearby American Athletic Club, where the middleweight, Mike Walsh, scoffed when he saw Nelson. By then Nelson had grown to his full 5 feet 7 ½ inches, but Walsh towered over him by half a foot and weighed at least twenty pounds more. "I'm not here to lick kids," he said.

Nelson knocked him out in six rounds and walked back to the pool hall to finish his game.

Nelson took two more boxing journeys. In the summer of 1902, at the age of twenty, he rode the underside of a freight car to Hot Springs, Arkansas. He fought there at least five times, but he made most of his money working as a waiter in a café. Soon, he bought the place in partnership with a man from out of town whom he didn't know. A few weeks later, the man absconded with Nelson's money. With a five-dollar bill he always kept in his shoe and a couple of leftover sandwiches, Nelson left Arkansas the way he had arrived, hanging on to the underside of a freight car. At Union Station in St. Louis, a train mechanic spotted him covered with soot and threatened to turn him over to police until Nelson identified himself. The train man had heard of him; he helped him clean up and pointed him toward a train to Chicago. That night, he spent most of the five dollars on a steak at the Flynn Brothers restaurant in the Loop, then got a bath and a good night's sleep at a flophouse on State Street.

In 1904, Nelson became nationally known fighting out of San Francisco. He knocked out Martin Canole, Eddie Hanlon, and Young Corbett. In the mining town of Butte, Montana, he met up with Aurelio Herrera, for whom he had worked just a year earlier in Chicago as a ten-dollar-a-week sparring partner. Herrera was an especially hard-hitting lightweight who had knocked out forty of his first fifty opponents. And he could take a punch. "Terrible Terry" McGovern said that striking Herrera's jaw "was just like hitting a Marvin safe."

Herrera enjoyed smoking black cigars and drinking whiskey, even during training and on the very day of a fight. Herrera had a cigar clamped between his teeth minutes before he and Nelson began their slugfest.

In the fourth round, Nelson claimed in his autobiography, Herrera hit him so hard that he turned a complete somersault, landing on his back. Herrera stood confidently, thinking the fight was over. To his surprise, however, Nelson bounced up and soon gained the advantage. After twenty rounds, the referee awarded him the decision.

Later in 1904, Nelson lost a twenty-round decision in San Francisco to the local favorite, Jimmy Britt, referred to there as Beau Brummell for his good looks and natty attire. Many cities had their own Beau Brummells, handsome white fighters, great white hopes. But the next year, Nelson knocked out Britt in the eighteenth round. After those battles, Nelson made news of a different sort. In an attempt to become "well-rounded," he made an unlikely visit to the Gardner Museum in Boston, knocking on the door of the Venetian-style palazzo on a cold February day and identifying himself to a big doorkeeper who reminded him of Jim Jeffries. Notified of Nelson's presence, Isabella Stewart Gardner sent word from upstairs that "a slight indisposition" would prevent her from meeting him, but that he was free to come in and look about. The *New York American* reported that he "rambled around among the art treasures without breaking any," and *The New York Times* could not resist making a page-one feature story of his "appreciation" of art.

But Nelson's boxing career was of greater importance to readers, and it was on the upswing. Noteworthy about many of his fights was his ability to wear down opponents—five of his bouts in 1904 ranged from sixteen to twenty rounds. He had never fought a fight to the finish, but he clamored for one. His forte was endurance, hence the nickname "the Durable Dane."

"I believe that all fights should be to a finish to determine which is the better man," he said.

Nelson claimed never to have had "more fun" than when he "licked a dozen negroes" during a melee that broke out after he had beaten a black boxer. Before knocking out another black man, he proudly quoted a friend who told him: "Go in and knock the devil's head off the coon. You don't hate him any more than I do."

As for Gans, Nelson regarded him with disdain. "All coons look alike to me," he said, borrowing the title of a popular song. To which he appended: "And this one I really want to clean."

14

Kid, you go home and go to bed tonight, we're gonna make the tryout tomorrow," Gans said almost offhandedly to Charlie Simms, a sparring partner, a week before the fight.

Gans had decided to find out how long he might be able to last in a fight to the finish. It was an outlandish idea. But what was his trainer, Frank McDonald, to do when Gans knew more about boxing than he did?

Even a century ago, a fighter would approach training with a conventional plan to build himself up gradually, and only rarely would he stray from the routine. Sparring, for instance, might include a modest number of rounds on certain days.

Not with Gans.

The next day, Simms went up to the second floor of Gans's hotel and found a private gaming room with all the tables and chairs pushed back to the walls. A makeshift ring had been set up. Shortly, a few men gathered, among them Rickard, the governor, and "Diamondfield" Jack Davis, a millionaire miner and gun-toting cowboy who had fought with Teddy Roosevelt's Rough Riders and barely escaped being hanged in Idaho in 1902 for a murder he didn't commit. Gans and Simms donned five-ounce gloves, lighter and more lethal than those worn almost ever since. "We didn't pull any punches, either," Simms said years later.

They fought thirty-five rounds.

"Then we put on four-ounce gloves, went outside, and boxed

twenty-five more rounds before twenty-five hundred people," Simms said. "They thought we were just starting. But that meant sixty rounds, a hundred and eighty minutes of fighting."

And it was hot. Despite its altitude, Goldfield had been struck by a heat wave that pushed temperatures close to one hundred degrees. Spectators sweated and suffered. It was worse for Gans and Simms. "Gans didn't have to tell me to go to bed that night," Simms said.

Those sixty rounds followed a hard twenty rounds Gans had fought shortly before going to Goldfield. Needing money, he agreed to meet Dave Holly for a bout on July 23 near Seattle. Holly, a black fighter from Philadelphia, was only a cut below championship level. Had he come along at a time when the lightweight division had less talent, he might have made a name for himself—he was that good. The pair had already fought four times, with Gans winning three, or perhaps two, with two draws—records vary. Their fifth fight was scheduled for Bainbridge Island, across Puget Sound, because prizefighting was banned in Seattle. It would be held in a barn on Pleasant Beach.

Antiprizefight groups beseeched the governor to intervene because previous bouts there had been so brutal, but he let the match proceed. It was a popular decision. So many fans turned out that half the crowd couldn't fit inside the barn. They spent the first few rounds shouting to be admitted. Five rounds in, some of those outside lifted a heavy timber and, using it as a battering ram, broke down one wall of the barn, which crashed onto dozens of people sitting in temporary bleachers on that side. No one was killed, but many suffered cuts and bruises.

Gans and Holly paused to consider the commotion, then resumed fighting. They even had to step over some shingles that had dropped from the roof into the ring.

The fight proved to be an ordeal for Gans. Holly broke through Gans's usually impenetrable defense in the early going, shoving him around and butting him above one of his eyes, opening a cut that bled for the rest of fight. But in the last ten rounds, Gans escaped Holly's swarming tactics often enough to box him and rally. In the eighteenth round, he closed one of Holly's eyes. At the end of the twentieth, Holly was hanging on. By then, each man was able to see the other with only one eye.

Gans won on points, but W. W. (Bill) Naughton, the dean of West Coast sportswriters, noted that a younger Gans would have knocked out Holly. Naughton suggested that Gans's long career (because many of his early fights went unrecorded, the total number of fights likely surpassed two hundred) had taken a toll on Gans. He looked fit, and he must have been in reasonably good condition because Holly was his sixth fight of 1906. But, to Naughton, there was something about Gans that wasn't right. Naughton decided that years in the ring had eroded Gans's skills.

Afterward, Gans announced that he would fight no more blacks, drawing the color line against his own race. He declared something that white fighters would never admit—that a potential black opponent could be hard to beat. "You don't get any credit if you lick 'em, and they are too tough to lick," Gans said.

George Siler, before being named to referee the Gans-Nelson fight, wrote several times in the *Chicago Daily Tribune* that Battling Nelson's manager, Billy Nolan, had told him that he considered Gans "too tough a proposition." But Siler believed Nolan never drew the color line because he knew that a Gans-Nelson fight would generate a great deal of money, if Gans could make the 133-pound weight limit. John L. Sullivan had proudly drawn the color line, and in retirement he urged every white fighter to do the same as he had. Prizefighting underscored the racism that permeated American life.

15

The fight set off a migration to Goldfield. The vanguard consisted of a motley group—the fight crowd. Included were sportswriters delighted to get out of their offices to go anywhere, even to the desert, and boxing's real cognoscenti: the managers, trainers, promoters, bucket carriers, and door watchers—the oracles of prizefighting. George Siler, the *Chicago Daily Tribune* sports editor, wired that he would soon be on his way to referee the fight; the best-known referee in the country, he would be paid five hundred dollars plus expenses.

Goldfield's hotels sold out immediately. To the question, Where would everyone else stay? the answer was, in tents they would have to pitch on the dusty plain. Or on somebody's floor. Or, if they had the right contacts, in a guest bedroom.

The Tonopah and Goldfield rail line went to work building three miles of siding on which two hundred Pullman cars could be parked. The Southern Pacific advertised a fight weekend special to Nevada from San Francisco for those who were still cleaning up from the earthquake and fire and who could afford the $27 round trip.

Schemers wired requests to take part in the festivities. A man from nearby Silver Peak, Nevada, offered to bring in thoroughbred racehorses from Emeryville, California, and stage a short meeting. Another, from Salt Lake City, wanted to put on a cockfight. A wrestler from New York who called himself Neromus asked if arrangements could be made for him to wrestle a bull.

Neither the desert's summer heat nor the vast wasteland to be traversed could deter fight fans. Two men from another Nevada mining camp spent three days walking across the desert, arriving footsore and covered with dirt.

Some Easterners contrived to ride free of charge on a Southern Pacific train bound for San Francisco by pretending to be part of a group of nonunion men being brought in to replace striking streetcar workers. At a stop in Nevada, the imposters jumped off and hid in the sagebrush until the train moved on, then hitched wagon rides to Goldfield.

A rogue named Wilson Mizner set out from New York to Goldfield to soak in the atmosphere of the Gans and Nelson fight camps after his brief marriage to Mrs. Charles T. Yerkes, known as "the forty-million-dollar widow," ended amid several disagreements, including one about his turning a wing of her mansion at Fifth Avenue and Sixty-fourth Street into a sumptuous boxing gym.

Bill Naughton, covering for the Hearst papers, ventured to Goldfield's outskirts to inspect the new seventy-two-hundred-seat stadium, built in a hollow bordering the town's graveyard, between downtown and the Tonopah and Goldfield rail station. He sized up the elevated ring, expressed amazement at the square structure with its parallel rows of planks extending more than twenty feet above the ground, and declared it the best boxing arena in the country. "It looks as if it would stand forever," he said.

The county sheriff announced that no guns would be allowed inside the sixteen-foot-high board fence. Exempt from that edict would be about twenty sheriff's deputies assigned to keep the peace.

Most of the special trains bound for the Gans-Nelson fight arrived at the Goldfield depot between midnight and 5:00 a.m. on the day of the fight, September 3. They came from Oakland,

Reno, Los Angeles, Chicago, and St. Paul. Some of the passengers said the journey was so uncomfortable they would never do any such thing again, no matter the attraction. The new Goldfield sidings almost filled up with one hundred and seventy-six Pullmans. From there, people, most of them in the dark, headed for the saloons.

The rowdy lead-up to most major fights usually ends at dawn on fight day, with the overnight hours taken up by speculation, hard drinking, and the sudden appearance of highly cosmeticized women. On this occasion, the notables, or the noticed, included Nan Patterson, a showgirl from the Broadway musical *Florodora*, who had been acquitted, after three sensational trials, of shooting and killing a former lover, the bookmaker and racehorse owner Caesar Young. She would shade herself from the sun with a hat of ostrich plumes.

The vaudevillian and actor Nat Goodwin, mingling with the fight crowd, met up with the moneyed George Graham Rice, with whom he went into business briefly, promoting mining stocks. Not all the mines existed, however, and Goodwin extricated himself from the partnership before Rice was arrested.

In Goldfield's swarming mob, counterfeit money was passed easily at the bars and gaming tables—ten-dollar bills with the same image on both sides went undetected in the hubbub. The Palace Gambling Pavilion was an exception. Cheats stayed away largely because its proprietor, John Lode, was as intimidating as any frontier presence; one writer described him as "the fattest faro dealer in the world."

Merchants watched their shops vigilantly because thieves had been breaking into back entrances on recent nights, filling their wagons with goods and escaping unseen. The crowd in the mining camp grew until there were more visitors at one time than had ever been known.

"A well nigh indescribable mixture of humanity surges abroad," the *Los Angeles Herald* reported. "Rough delvers of the soil elbow powerfully among Gotham millionaires . . . Women of the half world find their way . . . From the saloons and gambling houses comes a bright glare and sounds of revelry. Goldfield is fight mad and there'll be little sleep tonight."

The main streets were jammed, and no one seemed to care who had struck gold and for how much and who hadn't turned up anything—the talk was about the fight. It was about Nelson and how indestructible he appeared in his final workouts at the Ladies Aid Hall on Crook Avenue, how he breathed no harder after shadowboxing and skipping rope for forty-five minutes than if he'd been sitting in a chair all that time. Nelson had stamina; Spider Welsh, Martin Canole, and Eddie Hanlon had all pounded him in early rounds, but Nelson persevered in the punishment, wore them out, and won by knockout between the sixteenth and nineteenth rounds. As well, the talk was about "the colored boy" and how long he had been in the fight business but that he could still hit so awfully hard that some of his punches dug deep into the big bag out at the Merchants Hotel, leaving impressions in that bag and in their minds. He looked powerful enough to knock out a heavyweight.

Two men wagered their shares of stock in a mine, the winner to gain controlling interest in the property.

A Chicago man bet $10,000 on Gans to a Pittsburgh man's $8,000 on Nelson.

To emphasize his resolve, Gans announced that he had given Larry Sullivan power of attorney, which included the right to bet his entire end of the purse on him to win. "If I lose," Gans said, "I go out of Goldfield a pauper"—although he was a pauper already.

To a friend in New York, Gans wired assurance that he would win and encouraged the man to bet all he could. This he did, hurrying to the Metropole Hotel near Times Square, where gamblers gathered, and there he found plenty of action among Nelson backers.

Telegraph lines stretching to the most distant parts of the country would bring news of the fight from Goldfield. In cities from coast to coast, people planned to gather in front of telegraph or newspaper offices to follow the round-by-round progress. At *The San Francisco Call*, brief summaries of each round would be printed in large letters on white paper and pasted to a forty-foot-long board on the Market Street side of the building. In Maine, a *Bangor Daily News* staffer would be stationed on the top floor of the building to shout the latest bulletins to people in the street. *The Washington Times* announced in its pages: "Washingtonians interested in the bout will be kept informed of each and every detail of the preliminary incidents and of each blow struck in the big battle by a young man with a big voice, who will call out the returns through a megaphone from the third story of The Times building."

At the Presidio Hospital in San Francisco, ailing servicemen pooled their money and paid ten dollars to have a special telegraph service installed in a wardroom. The Kenneth Donnellan brokerage company at 490 California Street in San Francisco, which also had an office in Goldfield, scheduled a party for clients and prospective clients to hear fight bulletins over its own private line. All across the United States, private lines would be ordered.

Bat Masterson, the lawman turned sportswriter, wrote in the *New York Morning Telegraph* that Nelson was making a mistake fighting Gans because if Nelson lost, his earning power in vaudeville, $1,000 to $1,500 a week, would be reduced if not ruined. Masterson suspected Gans had declined, but guardedly picked him.

In other prefight stories, reporters—and the copy editors who wrote the headlines—continued to use derogatory terms when referring to Gans. Under the headline WHITE AND NEGRO AWAIT HOUR OF BITTER STRUGGLE, the *Los Angeles Herald* reported that "Goldfield people have taken a strong liking to the dingy." The secondary headline to one of the articles in *The Salt Lake Herald* read GOLDFIELD HAS PICKED DINGE AS WINNER OF TODAY'S BATTLE; and its reporter wrote that betting favored "the Smoke."

There were rumors, as there are before almost all major fights: The local sheriff would cancel the bout. Both fighters had been doped. Nolan warned that a group of San Francisco men who bet heavily on Gans had "something up their sleeves" that boded ill for Nelson, although what it might be Nolan didn't know.

From Nelson came indictments of Gans: He was not a "game" fighter. And: "There will be crepe in Coontown on Labor Day."

There was another rumor: Gans would have the fight fixed.

"If it isn't a fair and above-board fight—well, I hate to contemplate the result," Senator George Nixon said. "Nevada wouldn't be big enough for Nelson and Gans and the men who have arranged to bring them together in the ring."

"If Gans does not fight on the square he may never get out of the mining camp alive," W. J. Slattery wrote in *The San Francisco Call*.

An article that ran in the *Fairbanks* (Alaska) *Evening News* was even more ominous. The piece had no byline, and the dateline was misspelled as "Goldfields." The content was chilling. It said that if Gans fixed the fight there would be "'coon fruit' hanging from a telegraph pole in the morning."

16

At 11:25 on the morning of the fight, Larry Sullivan drove Gans from the Merchants Hotel to the arena. A caravan of autos and horse-drawn wagons followed, churning dust from the road. The fight could be bollixed up before it was to begin if Gans were late for Nolan's demand of three weigh-ins. Sullivan pulled up next to a tent behind the stands, and Gans went inside to await the first weigh-in at noon. Nelson settled into another tent.

Three weigh-ins were unheard of then, as they are now. A weigh-in generally occurs the day before the fight. It's done that way for the safety of the fighters. If a fighter is having difficulty making weight for a particular division, as Gans was in getting under the lightweight limit, he has time after weighing in to rehydrate and take some nourishment. The last thing Nolan was thinking of was Gans's well-being.

Already, the weigh-in had become an event in itself, a photo opportunity and a chance for predictions, boasts, and loose talk. Gans and Nelson would be weighed on a standard doctor's office balance-beam scale, which had been placed in the ring. The bar was set at 133 pounds, the limit for lightweights. If the beam remained steady when each boxer stepped on, it meant his weight was 133 or less. To conform to Nolan's demands, Gans had to weigh less, since he wore his gloves, trunks, and shoes, although a boxer usually stands on the scale barefooted and need wear only trunks, if that.

At noon, first Gans, then Nelson stepped on. Neither tipped the beam. Gans had turned away momentarily and was not watching when Nelson weighed in. Nolan refused Gans's request to have Nelson weigh again. Nolan then said something that annoyed Gans and prompted an uncharacteristically sharp response aimed at Nelson: "I'll attend to you when you get in the ring . . ."

Back in his tent, Gans rested on a cot and limited his intake to a few sips of water until the 1:30 weigh-in. Then, for the second time, neither fighter made the beam move. Several photographers snapped pictures of Gans and Nelson, and others gathered near the scale. After the second weigh-in, Nelson felt confident enough to eat a small dish of applesauce.

By then, prefight amusements in town—a rock drilling contest, footraces for both women and children—were finished. The mines for hundreds of miles around were closed; they had never been closed before, not even on Sundays. A twenty-piece firemen's band played from the balcony of the Miners' Union Hall as people began tramping out of town toward the arena. Some of the early arrivals hoped to pick up a tidbit that might inform their betting. There was a line to buy $5 grandstand tickets, which had been held in reserve; all other seats, priced up to a steep $25 ringside, had been sold.

The crowd included as many as three hundred women, a rarity outside of New York City, because Rickard promoted prizefighting as a suitable diversion for all adults—with an eye toward profits. He knew, with a promoter's instinct, that a woman had to be escorted, and that meant the sale of two tickets rather than one. And in a departure, children would be welcome, too—even more sales.

There was only one notable objection: The pastor of the local Presbyterian church threatened to expel any member of his congregation who attended the fight.

At three o'clock, Gans and Nelson were back in the ring for

the third weigh-in. With fight time approaching, the arena was almost full. Nelson stepped on the scale and met the limit. Now it was Gans's turn. Nolan and Rickard paid close attention. Rickard would have no choice but to pay Nelson more money if Gans was over the limit. The crowd was in no mood to have the fight canceled, and neither was Rickard, with almost a full house of paying customers, surely a record gate. Gans's paper-thin black shoes were tied not with laces but almost weightless strings. He wore no socks. He had calculated down to the ounce that he would not be overweight.

And he was not.

A telegraph operator had set up a working area at the nearby train depot. After every round, copyboys could rush ringside reporters' typed pages to him, and he would tap out the news almost as fast as it happened.

Moments before the fight, a telegram from Gans's mother arrived from Baltimore: JOE, THE EYES OF THE WORLD ARE ON YOU. EVERYBODY SAYS YOU OUGHT TO WIN. PETER JACKSON—a Baltimore middleweight and friend of Gans's—WILL TELL ME THE NEWS AND YOU BRING BACK THE BACON.

"Bring back the bacon." Within weeks, "bring *home* the bacon" cropped up in sports pages and in conversation and, in time, in literature. P. G. Wodehouse, for one, used it. The expression, long dormant, became fixed in the language.

17

The temperature topped one hundred degrees as Gans and Nelson climbed up to the ring. Gans held an umbrella above his head to protect himself from the sun. In both corners, aides took charge of holding umbrellas above the fighters. The fighters confined themselves to the cones of shade.

The sun beat down from a cloudless sky. Heat shimmered off the desert floor. The air was so hot it seemed as if it could turn reality inside out and make wide-open space feel claustrophobic. You almost had to concentrate to breathe.

A slight, warm breeze offered a little respite. In ringside seats, men discarded their suit coats but still looked overdressed in white shirts and ties. Women wore long, loose-fitting dresses light in color.

The referee, George Siler, mustachioed and sixty, also shed his suit coat. He wore gray trousers and, like those at ringside, a white shirt and tie. If not for a protective straw hat, and his necktie tucked into his shirt, he would have looked like a businessman going to a meeting.

Rickard noticed some empty seats high up in the stands and saw a gathering of men, poor men who had failed to strike it rich, standing outside the tall wooden gate. They hoped to follow the fight's progress from the crowd's reaction. Wanting to fill all the seats so as to ensure that his promotion looked as successful as it actually was, Rickard climbed atop the fence and raised his hands for silence. "Come on in—everybody," he shouted, and as the gate opened, the men surged in and the seats were filled.

The fighters wore robes. Nelson's was plain. Gans's was patterned, a robe that he had worn for other fights. The ring was demarcated by two strands of rope strung from corner post to corner post. Nolan claimed that Gans's hands should have been wrapped three hours earlier—hands are wrapped with cloth strips to prevent broken bones—so he could have been weighed each time with them. But Nolan was not going to distract Gans with the start of the fight minutes away. "I don't want any tape, anyway," Gans said.

He would fight without the wrappings despite the chance of having one of the small bones in his hands broken. Nelson's hands were wrapped.

Gans looked calm. He leaned over the top rope and spoke to someone in the first row. To another, he extended his gloves and shook hands. Gans had on light blue trunks, Nelson pale green.

Nelson had anticipated that Gans would weigh in wearing light shoes, and he did not expect those shoes to last more than a couple of rounds. He thought Gans would have a second pair brought to the ring and, beforehand, had asked Siler to disqualify Gans if his corner men took more than the minute allowed between rounds to fit him with different shoes. Siler wrote in his Chicago column that the crowd would not stand for a disqualification because of shoes. "That would mean a riot and probably bloodshed, and I don't intend taking my life in my hands. I am not afraid of getting filled full of pellets, but I am not inviting it."

There was no sign of a second pair of shoes.

But Gans did bring something else. He had an aide carry $2,000 in cash to the ring to make a side bet with Nelson on the outcome, and he interrupted Siler's final instructions to wager his $2,000 against Nelson's $1,200—and he would trust Nelson to get the money and pay up later. But, speaking for his fighter, Nolan declined the bet.

Siler flipped a coin to determine the fighters' corners. Gans called heads and won the right to choose the southwest corner, putting the sun at his back.

Gans told reporters that he would not accept anyone from his corner throwing in a towel or sponge, signaling surrender, and said he would lose only by knockout or if Siler asked him if he'd had enough and he concurred. Nelson said the same rules applied to him.

The fighters, posing for photographs close to the ropes, touched gloves. Nelson had two cauliflower ears—the left was more pronounced—and an ego, so that he always tried to pose with his better side to the camera. In this case, he succeeded.

Moments later, Gans and Nelson returned to their corners. As they awaited the opening bell, their seconds fanned them with towels.

•

Rickard had picked Miles Bros., a San Francisco firm, to film the fight. The company had established itself in the nascent film industry before its office was destroyed in the earthquake. The Miles brothers—there were four, including the principals, Harry and Herbert, who were twins—had a sense of history. They would mail a copy of their film of the fight to the Library of Congress.

Rickard had overruled the suggestion that a canvas covering be spread above the ring to shade the fighters because he realized that sunlight was essential for a clear film. As far as he was concerned, Gans and Nelson could suffer. There was money to be made. And Rickard would make it. He and Nolan would control the rights to have the film distributed.

The Miles brothers set their single camera relatively close to the ring, about fifty feet back and fifteen rows up in the stands, Gans to the right in the near corner, Nelson to the left in the far corner. The brothers had filmed one fight, Nelson's knockout of Jimmy Britt the previous September in Colma, California, south of San Francisco. But the camera had been located so far from the ring that the fighters looked small on film. Still, the result had its appeal.

"There is a wonderful fascination about the pictures of the Battling Nelson–Jimmy Britt fight which I cannot explain," Sam Austin, a columnist for *The National Police Gazette*, wrote. "Night after night I have sat in front of the big white curtain watching with interest the recurring episodes which transpired during the memorable battle. There is something which impresses the beholder after it is all over."

Even the act of filming itself, the sight of a camera, was a novelty to the spectators at Goldfield. The cameraman shouted for them to stand, turn toward him, and wave their hats or handkerchiefs. Happily, they did. Women waved parasols. The panorama included well-dressed men and women, several African Americans, prospectors identifiable by their boots and khaki-colored clothes, and a few children.

"There are about three hundred deputy sheriffs in this town to preserve order and to be on the outlook for trouble," Larry Sullivan, master of ceremonies, announced to the crowd. "I warn you all against jumping into the ring during or after the fight." Those deputy sheriffs stationed inside the arena were obvious. They kept their vests open for easy access to their pistols, and for effect.

Sullivan took a swig from a bottle of water in Gans's corner before addressing the crowd further. He had thought to invite the president of the United States, knowing that Roosevelt enjoyed boxing. But on that day, Roosevelt occupied himself with an even greater passion than boxing. He reviewed forty-five ships of the Atlantic fleet at Oyster Bay, New York, near his Sagamore Hill summer estate—a display that reminded fellow citizens that under his presidency the United States had become a world power.

Sullivan announced that he had invited Roosevelt but had not received a response.

Word was that Theodore Roosevelt, Jr., a son of the president, was in attendance, and Sullivan called his name. Someone shouted, "Show yourself and turn your face toward the moving pictures."

No luck. Teddy, Jr., wasn't there.

Sullivan settled for reading a telegram from John L. Sullivan, who expressed regret that he could not attend the fight, and introducing a number of senators and governors from western states. He called for three cheers for Rickard for arranging the fight, and the crowd responded heartily.

Nelson bounced, and banged his gloves together. Gans stood motionless as his seconds cooled him by rubbing down his chest and back with water. The background noise—an expectant hum from the crowd—continued to rise, and there were outbursts of shouts and cheers, like sparklers before a thunderous holiday celebration.

The umbrellas shading Gans and Nelson were folded.

The men who had been fanning the fighters scurried from the ring.

Gans was the betting favorite, 10 to 7.

It was 3:23 p.m.

The bell sounded and the crowd roared.

18

Nelson charged from his corner, as he did every fight. Gans held his ground and ducked slightly as Nelson threw a big hook that swept above his head. Almost comically, as if pointing his opponent in the direction of his target, Gans tapped two lefts to Nelson's head. He seemed to say, "I'm over here, friend," in as civilized an introduction as a boxer could make. Then he got serious: He unleashed a hail of rights and lefts to Nelson's face, landing punches repeatedly from a distance and close range. Nelson fell into a clinch.

Midway in the round, Gans doubled up with two rights to the jaw and a left to the face—a *three*-punch combination. All three punches hit hard. In the final moments of the round, the Associated Press reported that Gans "peppered Nelson's face with triphammer rights and lefts and kept this up until the gong rang . . . Gans went to his corner with a big lead. Blood flowed from Nelson's ears."

It didn't seem possible that Gans could box any better. But he did. In the second round, again fighting at long range, Gans scored almost at will. He landed a *five*-punch combination to the jaw—two right uppercuts, two lefts, and a straight right hand. Boxers who can deliver blows so rapidly have always been rare.

Nelson was helpless against such hand speed. But the AP noted that he seemed almost impervious to the punishment he had taken. So after two rounds, the odds, which could fluctuate during a fight because betting was allowed as it progressed, held steady. Questions about Gans lingered: How many rounds could he last, how much endurance could he have when past his prime? Could he keep punching hard? Bat Masterson had written in the *New York Morning Telegraph* that lately Gans had "not shown any of his old-time hitting qualities."

Gans had taken advantage of his seventy-one-inch reach, exceptional for a lightweight. At long range, he could extend his arms and easily box Nelson, whose reach was three and a half inches shorter.

In the third round, Nelson changed tactics. He began to stalk Gans, taking punishment as he did, but closing in relentlessly, pressuring, using his elbows to lock Gans's arms next to his body so he couldn't swing, negating his reach. For his effort, though, Nelson took an especially sharp right to the ear, after which he grabbed and held.

For his part, Gans looked comfortable changing his own tactics, fighting at close range and keeping his movement to a minimum, conserving energy while blocking and dodging punches. Some of the punches Gans dodged barely missed, but narrowly avoiding catastrophe was one of his trademarks—like a race car driver roaring across the finish line with a thimbleful of gas. On the attack, he found his target as effectively as he had from a distance, only now he used uppercuts and counterpunches. He drew blood from Nelson's nose with a straight left as they traded punches at midring. But after the round, the AP carried an ominous, double-edged synopsis: "Nelson is being outpointed, but he never gives ground and seems to thrive on Gans's punches."

Jack London had Nelson pegged perfectly: He *was* a brute. He ignored pain. His face was cut, his ears bled, his blood spilled to the ring floor. But he was single-minded in carrying the fight to Gans and trying to wear him down. Starting in the fourth round, Nelson began to roughhouse. He shoved Gans, caught up with him, and shoved him some more. He thrust his left shoulder upward, resulting in a jolt to the chin. As he waded in, he held his hands alongside his face, as if battling a storm.

Gans was known for blocking a left-hand lead, then throwing a straight right. Nevertheless, Nelson occasionally managed to land his left hand on Gans's jaw. Gans countered, jabbing and scoring. Nelson repeatedly pushed Gans to the ropes, hitting him with both hands. His aggressiveness, which included low blows, created the impression that the fourth round was about even. Nelson drew applause as he returned to his corner. Incongruously, he smiled faintly through his blood-smeared face.

Gans, however, left no doubt as to the winner of rounds five through eight. He dug his gloves brutally into Nelson's face and body. His punches snapped Nelson's head back. They landed on the nose, spraying blood. Gans worked gracefully, as if hitting a light bag in training. After the fifth round, Nelson went to his corner spitting blood. And after the sixth, the AP reported: "Nelson was in bad shape when he took his chair. His face was cut to ribbons and Gans looked like a sure winner."

In the seventh round, Nelson continued to force Gans around the ring, but Gans staggered him with blows to the head that sent more blood streaming from his nose and mouth. Gans opened a cut near Nelson's left eye. The cut troubled Nelson, and it would continue to trouble him.

Yet he never stopped running into punches—never, that is, until late in the eighth round. That's when Gans dropped him like a plumb line.

Gans landed two quick blows to the head, a right and a left, and Nelson fell to his knees. His gloves hit the canvas in front of him. He stayed frozen for an instant, as if in prayer. Gans stood behind him as Siler moved in, about to count. But he didn't have time. Nelson jumped to his feet, turning counterclockwise to face Gans, who punished him more until, at the bell, Nelson was all but knocked out. He stumbled to his corner and sat down hard. Gans turned and walked away quickly. He showed no emotion.

For years to come, the first eight rounds would serve as a blueprint, or at least a mental outline, for boxers and trainers. They took their cues from Gans's repertoire, learning mostly by word of mouth or by reading how Gans picked apart Nelson with precision punching and, in turn, swatted away Nelson's blows with his gloves and forearms, how Gans waited patiently for openings, avoided Nelson's swings, counterpunched.

·

Watching from the grandstand in Goldfield, one might have thought there was no one, no matter the weight class, who ever approached Gans's understanding of boxing, or his inventiveness. And that may have been true. But even the greatest Renaissance artists apprenticed under a master. And Gans had one.

Long before, a slender black youth went to the fights in Baltimore to watch an expert in action. Bob Fitzsimmons was middleweight champion of the world and was on course to become heavyweight champion and, later, light heavyweight champion— the first man to win three titles. His looks were unusual for a boxer, and the sight of him in a ring took some getting used to. Amused boyhood friends said he was "a cadaverous-looking kid." He was pale and balding, his head small and bullet-shaped. What hair he had was red. He was about six feet tall, but his legs were disproportionately long and thin; John L. Sullivan said Fitzsimmons looked as if he stood on stilts. When he disrobed in the ring, his chalk-colored body, which was dotted with freckles, often elicited laughter. In a sport that liberally affixes nicknames to fighters, Robert Prometheus Fitzsimmons collected an abundance of them. He was known as "Ruby Robert," "Freckled Bob," "Speckled Bob," "Ruddy Bob," "the Freckled Wonder," "Great

Fitz," "Fighting Fitz," "the Kangaroo," "the Antipodean," and "Lanky Bob."

But Fitzsimmons's odd physique included a barrel chest and powerful arms. His back rippled with muscles. He had the strength of a blacksmith; he had grown up as one in New Zealand. When he was nine years old, his parents moved there from Cornwall, England—hence another nickname, "the Cornishman." His work at the forge developed his chest and shoulders, and he beat up several youngsters who were apprenticed to blacksmiths. In 1880, he knocked out four opponents to win an amateur tournament. Soon after, he beat five men in one night. In 1883, at the age of twenty, he moved to Australia and began a professional boxing career, fighting successfully with bare knuckles and gloves. In February 1890, in Sydney, he met a good middleweight named Jim Hall. Fitzsimmons was the better fighter, but the bout would haunt him for the rest of his life. He was so heavily favored that bookmakers stood to lose money. One of them demanded that he throw the fight, threatening that he would not be paid unless he did. Fitzsimmons took a dive in the fourth round.

"What was I to do?" he said. "I had spent every cent I possessed in training and paying my helpers . . . I was flat broke. The temptation was too much, and I yielded . . . How often I have yearned to go back and blot it out. "

Hall subsequently got into a bar brawl and suffered knife wounds, preventing him from sailing to America to pursue the middleweight championship, as had been arranged by Australian promoters. Instead, they named Fitzsimmons to make the trip, and he took just three fights—three knockouts—to get a shot at the middleweight championship. Jack Dempsey, known as "the Nonpareil"—the original Jack Dempsey, who held the title—shrugged off the possibility of losing to such an odd-looking character. But on January 14, 1891, in New Orleans, Fitzsimmons knocked down Dempsey thirteen times in thirteen rounds—the last time, for the count.

Two years later, Hall caught up with Fitzsimmons in New Orleans, and they had their rematch. Fitzsimmons knocked him out in four rounds. A telltale right uppercut to the chin traveled only inches. The short punch was a Fitzsimmons trademark.

Then came the evening that would all but guarantee greatness for Gans: the night of May 30, 1893, when he saw Fitzsimmons fight in Baltimore. Fitzsimmons knocked out Jack Warner in the first round. Afterward, Fitzsimmons remained in the city to give exhibitions, and the young Gans began to show up at the champion's daily workouts. He was fascinated by Fitzsimmons, recognizing him to be a master strategist. It wasn't easy for anyone to break into Fitzsimmons's consciousness. Fitzsimmons disliked distractions. He preferred to train in private. But he was impressed with Gans's intelligence, his sinewy build, and his promising skills, which Caleb Bond had begun to develop.

Gans's skin color did not concern Fitzsimmons. "The only trait for which his worst enemy can criticize him," philanthropist and publisher A. J. Drexel Biddle wrote in an introduction to Fitzsimmons's book *Physical Culture and Self-Defense*, "is that of his unbounded generosity." Fitzsimmons argued consistently against white fighters drawing the color line, saying that their achievements would be tainted if they excluded black fighters.

Almost daily, he provided the young Gans with a tutorial. They talked and sparred. Fitzsimmons passed on techniques he had learned from Jim Corbett, considered the father of modern boxing. In knocking out John L. Sullivan, Corbett became the first heavyweight champion under the new Marquess of Queensberry rules—the guidelines of modern boxing, calling for gloves and three-minute rounds with one-minute intervals. Corbett had broken the mold of simply slugging by introducing offensive and defensive tactics. He approached the sport scientifically. The New York *World*'s Hype Igoe (the newspaper's editor, Herbert

Bayard Swope, had decided that his boxing writer, also named Herbert, needed a more eye-catching handle) described Corbett as "the immaculate stylist who put the high silk hat on The Manly Art of Self Defense."

When Fitzsimmons knocked out Corbett in fourteen rounds in 1897 to become the first English-born gloved heavyweight champion—and the last for a century—he simply followed Corbett's approach, blocking punches and saving energy by striking only when he saw an opening. Fitzsimmons was the sport's best thinker up to that point. He knew exactly what kind of punch he wanted to throw long before the opportunity presented itself. He had determined that the body could provide the leverage to knock out even a bigger man, and, at 156½ pounds, he gave away thirty pounds to Corbett.

His most famous punch was a hard left hand to the midsection just below the breastbone—the solar plexus punch.

Gans followed Fitzsimmons's principles. His style was ahead of its time, distinctly twentieth century. He did not stand straight up; he leaned forward but remained balanced, kept his elbows in, and rounded his shoulders so that he was both ready to defend and coiled to attack with straight hitting. He always hit hard—that came to him naturally—and while he was not known primarily as a knockout artist, he was one; as his knockout of Frank Erne proved, he could end a fight with one punch. But he was known more for his defense, the part he studied the most and tried to perfect because he could never forget being taught that he could be hurt if surprised. He blocked punches and, like Fitzsimmons, avoided punches by bobbing his head and moving only inches, although if necessary he could move farther. With defense foremost in mind, he would search patiently for an opening, sometimes so patiently his fans became impatient.

In one of his early bouts in Baltimore, people hissed him because they thought he was taking too long—a round and a half—to stop one Billy Young. Gans explained after the fight that no opponent should be taken lightly. And to him that included someone as bedraggled-looking as Young, a veteran who removed his false teeth before the opening bell.

"Joe never threw a punch unless he was sure it would land on a vital spot," Harry Lenny, a frequent sparring partner, said. "He had the spots picked out, mentally marked in big red circles on his opponent's body: the temple, the point of the chin, the bridge of the nose, the liver, the spleen, the solar plexus. He'd pick out one or two of these points and maneuver his opponent until he left a clear opening. It was a thing of beauty to watch Joe in the ring."

19

Nelson rallied in the ninth round, and he continued his come-back in the tenth and eleventh rounds. His rage was obvious as he flailed away. He landed four punches to Gans's one. When one of his handlers shouted, "Stay with him, don't let him get away," he practically overwhelmed Gans. In taking the momentum, Nelson, not surprisingly, held Gans and head-butted him. Siler, the referee, let it go. He chose not to disqualify Nelson because he wanted the crowd to get its money's worth.

But in the twelfth round, as Nelson drove Gans to the ropes, he lost his footing and slipped to the floor. Gans towered above him. Siler stood aside. The rules did not require Gans to step back or for Siler to rub clean Nelson's gloves. There were no nice-ties in boxing, and there still are few. Gans looked down at his opponent. Nelson's unprotected jaw invited what would have been a legal punch. Gans had plenty of room to swing, more room by far than he ever needed. Usually, he could find a space where one didn't seem to be. Now, he could have swung any way he cared to, and driven his fist into Nelson's mealy face.

But Gans restrained himself. Instead, in a sportsmanlike ges-ture, a humble act, really, he put out his right hand to help Nel-son to his feet. Nelson accepted Gans's graciousness. He took Gans's hand.

Yet midway through the twelfth, Nelson extended his cranium, as A. J. Liebling might have put it. So much for graciousness.

And later in the round, Nelson again lowered his head and rammed Gans's face, bloodying his mouth. In the thirteenth round, Nelson did it again. Despite the fouls, Gans won those two rounds. He boxed almost as beautifully as he had early in the fight, and now he managed to do it even as Nelson continued to lunge into him and foul him.

Nelson was so violently awkward that, in the fourteenth round, he missed a haphazard punch and swung himself backward through the ropes. He landed in a sitting position on the ring apron, his legs draped over the lower rope into the ring. Again, Gans stood directly above him. Again, Gans offered his hand.

This time Nelson responded angrily. He sprang to his feet and hit Gans when his guard was down.

"Gans chivalrously pulled him back to the ring," the Associated Press reported. "As a reward for this act of courtesy the Dane smashed Gans on the body, and the crowd yelled its disapproval."

Gans offered no protest. He had been treated worse.

•

On May 18, 1897, Gans met Mike Leonard of Brooklyn in a tenrounder in San Francisco. Jim Jeffries, the future heavyweight champion, was on the undercard, fighting for only the fifth time in his career. Gans-Leonard was the attraction. Leonard would never gain the fame of other Leonards, as Benny or Sugar Ray. But at the time, he was Brooklyn's Beau Brummell, its white hope.

In June 1894, he boxed six rounds with Jack Cushing in an almost empty room in West Orange, New Jersey. Only a few people were there—and a kinetoscope, an early film camera. Each round was limited to one minute—that was the maximum length of time a kinetoscope could function. Seven minutes were allowed to elapse between rounds so the machine could be prepared to continue. Two months later, Leonard was back in the news as the Kinetoscope Exhibiting Company opened a parlor at 83 Nassau Street in downtown Manhattan expressly to show the film of his victory. Customers had to peer inside six boxes, one box per round, five cents a box.

Like Nelson, however, Leonard was prejudiced against blacks. And he didn't hesitate to break the rules of the ring. On September 23, 1895, he fought in Baltimore against a local man named Charles Gehring. In the third round, he grabbed Gehring around the neck with his left hand, pulled him forward, and pounded a right uppercut to the jaw. A riot ensued. A beer bottle sailed over the ring, followed by a rush of Gehring's angry fans, Gehring's manager leading the way until Leonard stopped him with a right to the jaw. Police restored order and the referee ruled no contest.

In San Francisco, fight fans thought Gans and Leonard were friends. They had arrived on the same train. They had agreed to split $2,000 evenly. The fight was rumored to be fixed. Western fans did not trust eastern fighters, especially a black fighter. And the sponsoring Olympic Club cautioned against betting because Leonard was overweight and for "other reasons" that were not explained.

But San Francisco was a fight town, and on fight night its fans seemed to forget all the warning signs. They turned out hoping to see an honest fight. Twenty-five hundred, most of them men wearing suits and ties, filled Woodward's Pavilion in the Mission District. Hundreds more clamored to get in. At the referee's signal, the fighters walked to the center of the ring for final instructions.

Leonard spat in Gans's face.

Gans didn't move. Nor did he change expression.

"There was an angry demonstration from the crowd, which

did not subside for the minute," *The Brooklyn Daily Eagle* said, "but Gans kept cool and seemed satisfied to await his opportunity for wiping out the insult."

Of all the things that Gans learned from Fitzsimmons, maybe the most important was restraint. Fitzsimmons had simply copied Corbett, who deserved to be called "Gentleman Jim," while Corbett had taken his manners from nineteenth-century English boxers. Fitzsimmons believed in fighting fairly and in being as polite as possible. When he came to Baltimore in 1893 and scored a first-round knockout, he bent over his opponent and helped him to his corner. Two years earlier, Fitzsimmons backed away several times during his one-sided victory over Jack Dempsey, "the Nonpareil," hoping the referee would stop the bout. Once, the fallen Dempsey implored Fitzsimmons to help him to his feet, which Fitzsimmons did. In the words of Fitz's friend Drexel Biddle, he "placed Dempsey upright."

Once, after knocking down George Scott, the boxing instructor at the Olympic Club in New Orleans, while sparring, Fitzsimmons picked him up and kissed him on the cheek. One night in Chicago, Fitzsimmons knocked out two opponents, one after the other. Fitz carried the first to his corner and assisted in reviving the second, who by one account had fallen "like a dead man."

Gans beat Leonard decisively over ten rounds. San Franciscans cheered him throughout. The same thing would happen in Goldfield. In both places, predominantly white crowds sided with the black man. They objected to unfairness. They booed Leonard; they booed Nelson. But there is no evidence that the reaction affected Leonard, and Nelson clearly ignored it. He dominated the fourteenth round. And after the bell, he glared at Gans, and swung at him. This time Gans did lose his composure. He swung back. Both fighters missed with their punches. Crazily, Nelson kicked at Gans. Gans kicked at him. Again, both missed.

This was one of the few times—maybe the only time—that Gans failed to maintain the calm that helped define him as a boxer.

The handlers from both corners rushed to their men and hurried to part them. During the minute's rest, Gans settled down. And in the fifteenth round he rallied again—not before taking an elbow to the face and a head butt that was so hard it seemed even to startle Siler. The referee tapped Nelson on the shoulder and shouted for him to stop butting. The warning, like the others before it, went unheeded. Nelson leaned on Gans and tied him up. They wrestled toward Nelson's corner. As they did, Gans slipped free for the first time in a long time. He slid off the ropes and shot a right hand to Nelson's face. The blow spun Nelson's head around, as if a nail had been driven into his cheek.

Nelson dropped to the floor. This was no flash knockdown, as in the eighth round. The punch was powerful enough to knock out most opponents. It was a heavyweight's punch. A Joe Louis could be expected to throw a punch that heavy. Yet a smaller man can deliver with power, too, in part from massing strength in his wrist and forearm, followed almost simultaneously by a sharp snap of the wrist. That's how Sugar Ray Robinson harnessed power. And Gans.

But Gans never fought anyone who could take a punch like Nelson.

Nelson was down. Siler began counting, whipping his right arm. But at the count of two—just two!—Nelson stood up.

What could put Nelson down and keep him down? Gans was not the first fighter to wonder, nor was he the last. Nelson stood shakily, brought to his feet by instinct. Gans, who had tripped over his outstretched opponent, stood behind him. The two were in Nelson's corner. As Nelson turned to his right, Gans hit him three times in the face. Nelson grabbed Gans and hung on. Seconds ticked away. The fifteenth round ended.

That was the traditional distance for championship fights during much of the twentieth century. Had that been the end, had there been scoring by rounds, Gans would have won easily: ten rounds to five, perhaps, or ten to four with one even. Instead, there was no hint of an ending.

20

In the sixteenth round at Goldfield, Gans needed the endurance that had come so easily in years past. He looked tired as he clinched with Nelson. Nelson tumbled backward between the ropes, pulling Gans after him. Spectators pushed them back into the ring, and they held each other some more. Three rights to the face from Nelson left Gans bloody. It was Nelson's round, and so was the seventeenth, although he hit Gans low and twisted his arm. Siler had no option other than to disqualify Nelson, but he still believed people would be unhappy to have him end the fight as early as the seventeenth round. Yet the opening bell had sounded more than an hour earlier. It was four-thirty in the afternoon.

Courage seemed to carry Gans in the eighteenth. He wobbled Nelson with two rights to the jaw. Like a matador, Gans stepped aside to give Nelson room to fall, but Nelson did not fall. Gans was rallying. In the nineteenth and twentieth rounds he shook Nelson several times with blows to the face. In turn, Nelson used his head as a weapon as much as his fists. Siler touched Nelson's head again, emphasizing that he wanted him to stop butting. Siler even grabbed Nelson's hair to try to make him stop. That didn't work either.

Late in the twentieth round, Gans landed punches easily. Nelson, still plodding forward, found himself in more trouble than the two times when he had been knocked down, in the eighth

and the fifteenth rounds. Gans sent a right to the jaw that typically knocked out others. Not Nelson. But the bell ending the
twentieth round likely saved him.

Nelson's tenacity, although not his tactics, rivaled that of Kid
McPartland, with whom Gans had fought an epic twenty-five-
rounder in 1898 in New York that brought Gans widespread acclaim. McPartland, like Gans an exquisite boxer, had barely lost
a twenty-five-round fight to Kid Lavigne when he was the lightweight champion. So on November 4, 1898, seventy-two hundred spectators filled New York's Lenox Athletic Club, at 107th
Street and Lexington Avenue, expecting McPartland to beat Gans.

As the fight developed, Gans did everything McPartland did,
only better. Gans reduced McPartland's eyes to slits. Like Nelson, however, McPartland would not give in, and he lasted the
full twenty-five rounds. Gans won by decision. If he had fought
more than 150 times, as he estimated—poor record keeping makes
his count difficult to verify—or even the 55 times listed in *The
Ring Record Book and Boxing Encyclopedia*, Gans had come to
fame late.

The next day's papers lauded his performance.

William Randolph Hearst's *Journal* said: "Never has there
been a truly clever boxer, a more thorough ring strategist, a better judge of distance and opportunity or a less excitable fighter
than Joe Gans, of Baltimore."

The more staid *Herald* wrote: "Now all the world knows what
Gans's friends have all along known—that the colored boy is
the cleverest fighter of his weight in the ring today."

•

Gans's emergence as a national figure coincided with that of
New York as a fight town. In 1896, the Horton law legalized
prizefighting in the state, and until the law was repealed in 1900,
several arenas in Manhattan featured boxing. Gans fought eight

times at the Broadway Athletic Club, at 728–730 Broadway in Greenwich Village. The largest of the city's clubs, it was an architectural curiosity with a castle-like stone front modeled after part of the Roman-built London Wall. The building looked as if it had materialized out of a fog.

Gans arrived in New York at a time when tens of thousands were immigrating there. Already, the population was three million. Gans liked the hurly-burly of the city, and the fact that many people there liked to dress up, as he did. Men wore dark suits and hats, women hats with flowers and veils and long skirts that they hiked up to prevent their hems from dragging in the dirt. Fruit and vegetable stands bottlenecked the narrow passageways of lower Manhattan. Frightened horses often ran away with their carriages.

An Irish immigrant paid a dime to see a horse that had been advertised as having its tail where its head should be, only to come face to rump with an animal turned backward in its stall. People wanted to be entertained, and they sat in the dark and watched stage shows—in 1896, there was only a single movie theater with a projector that beamed jerky images onto a screen. Boxing audiences grew with the sport's new cachet bestowed by the state legislature, and spectators in the choice seats became increasingly fashionable. The middle class and the rich dandies of Manhattan, their ladies on their arms, flocked to the Broadway Athletic Club and routinely joined the sporting crowd to fill its three thousand seats. It was the beginning of the age of fight-going in New York.

People could get close to the violence, hear the punches land, or maybe see a fallen fighter's quivering legs, yet be safe. The Broadway's ringside seats comprised six rows of folding chairs, and the rows of long benches behind them rose steeply to offer ideal views. Directly above the ring, a chandelier cast brilliant light on the fighters.

Gans fought sixteen times in Manhattan and Brooklyn from 1896 to 1900. He went twenty-five rounds five times; in all, he had gone twenty rounds or more fifteen times before stepping into the ring against Nelson. But his New York days were not entirely glorious. In October 1896, Gans journeyed by train to New York as a substitute in a fifteen-rounder against Dal Hawkins, a Jim Corbett protégé from San Francisco. Gans was advertised as unbeaten in thirty-two fights despite a loss to Johnny Van Heest on a racially biased decision and a loss in a little-noted four-rounder in 1894, when only medals were awarded. He lost a decision to a Baltimore fighter named Paul "the Kangaroo" Johnson; the next year, Gans redeemed himself by winning a ten-round decision over Johnson, a victory that would establish a pattern: No fighter who beat Gans in a first meeting would beat him a second time.

Interest in Hawkins-Gans was especially high because, with the Horton law in effect, fans no longer had to worry about a police raid. On October 6, before a packed house at the Bohemian Sporting Club, at Eighty-first Street and Amsterdam Avenue, Gans and Hawkins fought ten fairly even rounds before Gans appeared to pull ahead during the next five. At the finish, the crowd shouted "Draw! Draw!" and "Gans! Gans!" The referee, however, declared Hawkins the winner. Once again, racial bias, not an opponent, had done Gans in. As before, it was easier for the referee to favor a white boxer, this time one with Corbett in his corner, than a young black.

"It was an outrage to give such a decision after the way that Gans had fought Hawkins, and the crowd sympathized with Gans," the New York *World* reported.

The overwhelmingly white crowd's positive reaction to Gans in his first New York fight showed a respect for his ability. Spectators approved of his demeanor, which was businesslike and absent of flash. His appeal as a boxer had crossed racial lines. No doubt, sometime, somewhere in America, a white crowd had reacted similarly when the result of a mixed-race bout was announced. But Gans had fought in the nation's biggest city against a talent from the storied Olympic Club of San Francisco. For the first of many times on a national stage, Gans earned plaudits from a white audience. He would be the first African American after horse racing's early black jockeys and the cyclist "Major" Taylor whose athletic ability even hinted at the possibility, just the possibility, that sports could be a springboard for racial justice in American daily life.

Fair treatment of blacks was almost unheard of then, in the 1890s. John Tyler Morgan, an Alabama senator and former Confederate Army general, called for "a plan for the return of the negroes to Africa, the natural home of the race."

"Not only are the climatic conditions exactly suited to the negro," Morgan said in a speech in Washington, "but the products are to his liking, and not until he is on African soil will he be the equal of his Anglo-Saxon brother. In this country his color is a barrier to his practical equality, and no matter how educated or refined he may become he can never hope to associate with those of the white race."

From 1889 until the end of World War I, more than twenty-four hundred African Americans were hanged or burned at the stake, many of them accused of nothing more than making "boastful remarks" or seeking employment "out of place." In 1895, five blacks who helped build a rail line in South Texas were found hanged. In an unsigned newspaper article—many news stories contained opinion and were published without bylines, although in this case the author may have welcomed anonymity—a reporter decried the violence: "An investigation was made, but like all investigations in this country, nothing resulted. It was given out that they must have been murdered by robbers, but it is believed that they were pursued by the contractors and trapped and killed, so as not to allow them to escape. The life of the American Negroes at work here is terrible. Many have been beaten to death."

Few blacks escaped a lifetime of harassment, or, at the least, of being regarded as inferior. A United States congressman, Thomas Hardwick of Georgia, tried to have Gans evicted from the dining car of a train. "We can't do that, sir," the conductor replied. "Well if that fresh nigger gets near me I'm going to wipe the car up with him," Hardwick replied. "I won't have him around me." The congressman persisted in learning the black man's identity, but after he learned it, he said nothing.

In an 1898 encounter with a Baltimore policeman, Gans was charged with assaulting the officer and taken to court. The officer had no bruises, he told the judge, because he had dodged two punches thrown at him. "Your Honor," Gans responded, "I am a professional prizefighter. If I had swung at this officer, I would not have missed."

Guilty anyway! Gans paid a five-dollar fine.

•

Gans spent much of 1896 to 1900 in New York as boxing took hold there. His star power foretold that of Kid Chocolate and Beau Jack and Sugar Ray Robinson, and his Manhattan trilogy of 1899 with George "Elbows" McFadden—a loss, a draw ruled by the referee in a bout Gans appeared to win, and, finally, a victory that could not be denied—prefigured the Robinson–Jake La Motta, Ali–Joe Frazier serials.

When sportswriters discovered John McGraw, player-manager of the Baltimore Orioles and an acquaintance of Gans, visiting New York in March 1900, he told them he was there to attend a Gans title fight, his first with Frank Erne. Actually, McGraw was seeking a job with the New York Giants baseball club. That spring, fans flocked around Gans at Coney Island's Gravesend racetrack as Herford remained close by, smoking a cigar and feeling important.

Gans trained in New Jersey, running the roads among packs of boxers, and in Harlem, where he became the foremost fighter in Grupp's, a popular gym. One day, a photographer snapped Gans relaxing in a rocking chair next to a clapboard house. It made for a bucolic scene: Harlem as a country retreat.

He courted a dancer in the Williams and Walker black vaudeville company, befriending the comedian and singer Bert Williams so he could gain admittance to the company's shows by way of the stage door. Williams read Darwin and Goethe and Oscar Wilde, and he liked to box. Gans gave him lessons. An appreciative Williams inserted Gans into one of his most popular numbers, "I Think I See My Brother Comin' Home Right Now":

Josephus Gans,
He's got the easiest of plans,
Of makin' money
Dat Ah ever did see.
Ah'm matched next week,
Against the Terrible Greek,
Ah'm gonna fight till Brother Bill comes home.
Brother Bill's been dead now seventeen years,
And dead men seldom roam,
But Ah's layin'
Mah plans,
Like Josephus Gans,
Ah'm gonna fight till Brother Bill comes home.
Chorus: Ah thinks Ah sees mah brothah comin' home
*   right now . . .*

The entire Williams and Walker company turned out for Gans's wedding to Madge Wadkins on April 8, 1900. The ceremony took place at 23 West Fortieth Street in Manhattan, the home of her uncle, A. E. Warren. The crowd was so large that relatively few were able to see the vows exchanged, and two other houses on the block had to be taken over for the celebration. The wedding had been so glamorous that it crashed at least one major New York newspaper's society coverage, usually a white domain. JOE GANS WEDDED IN A BLAZE OF COLOR, *The World* announced in a headline the paper's editors no doubt considered clever. The same approach marked the lead of the article: "It was the darkest wedding and at the same time the most brilliant that New York has seen in many a day . . ." The bride's father, a wealthy Cincinnati businessman whose holdings included a Turkish bath, presented her with a dowry of $10,000, and was said by *The World* to be "delighted to have his daughter make so excellent a match."

Gans fought in New York right up to the repeal of the Horton law. He took part in a fight on February 9, 1900, at the Broadway Athletic Club—a fight *The New York Times* predicted would sound the "death-knell" of the law. Gans tried to dispose of his white opponent, Spike Sullivan of Boston, as gently as possible, but Sullivan always fought back. Finally, during the fourteenth round, as Gans was pounding at will, the referee stopped the fight to save Sullivan from further punishment. With that, one of Sullivan's seconds, a New York fighter named Dan Donnelly, jumped into the ring and knocked out the referee, Charlie White, with one punch. "Kick Donnelly's head off . . . Kill him!" fans shouted. Police took Donnelly to jail. White went to St. Vincent's Hospital, where six stitches closed a gash over his left eye.

Legislators denounced prizefighting for its brutality and lawlessness. Soon it would be shunted to back rooms and basements. Before then, however, Gans met Hawkins a second time. On May 25, 1900, at the Broadway Athletic Club, Hawkins dropped Gans with his good left hand and almost finished him, but in the second round Gans knocked out Hawkins with a right to the jaw. It was one of the best short fights ever, and it solidified Gans's standing among New York fans: He had rallied when hurt, the mark of a champion.

On August 31, 1900, they fought a third time, again at the Broadway A.C. This time, Gans knocked out Hawkins in the third round with another right to the jaw. With that, legalized boxing in New York became an off-again, on-again, off-again thing until 1920, when Governor Al Smith signed the Walker bill.

Between 1900 and 1920, matches often took place behind closed doors, and fans paid an admission fee, their so-called membership dues, which admitted them to the club. The big fights went elsewhere. Gans threw the last punch of the Horton era.

21

In the twenty-third round at Goldfield, Nelson fought as if he could go on until darkness fell and the sun came up. Gans had outboxed him the previous two rounds, and Nelson's left eye was swollen and his right eye bruised. But Gans's surprising endurance and his superior punching power went for naught. Nelson punished Gans with two rights to the face, two rights to the heart, and a flurry to the head. Gans staggered and did not fight back. Nobody watching the fight could be sure who would win, creating the suspense that promoters dream of. "Nelson, Nelson!" some fans shouted. The end seemed near for Gans when the bell came, this time, to *his* rescue. He had made it to the end of the twenty-third round. He had not always been so fortunate.

In New York, George "Elbows" McFadden had stopped him in the twenty-third round. They would fight six more times, and McFadden would prove almost as tough as Nelson: Gans would win four and he and McFadden would fight to two draws. But on April 14, 1899, at the Broadway Athletic Club, Gans went to the ring unprepared, despite claiming a year earlier how important it was not to underestimate any opponent. He underestimated McFadden. Much later, Gans owned up to enjoying the "primrose path" during the weeks before the fight. "I was staying up late at night, and in several ways conducting myself in a manner that is ruinous to a fighter," he said.

"As I didn't think very seriously of McFadden's ability as a fighter, there was absolutely no work done by me along training lines. I continued to hit it up until the very night of the fight, and was not only fat, but as slow as an ice wagon compared to my past speed." He blamed his defeat on "booze and late hours," and he also starved himself to make the 133-pound weight limit, and then gorged on, depending on the version, a whole custard pie or about two dozen doughnuts. He complained of stomach pain during the fight, and McFadden added to his woe. Years later, the New York columnist Dan Daniel wrote that "'Elbows' had hit Joe right in the pie."

At the time, some writers accused Gans of losing to McFadden intentionally. And they denounced him again for refusing to continue his first title fight with the champion Frank Erne on March 23, 1900, after an accidental head butt near his left eye in the twelfth round blinded him with his own blood. A cut on the eyelid or eyebrow is hard to fix, and most ringside accounts of that fight, also at the Broadway Athletic Club, said the cut was serious. After he told the referee "I quit," a distraught Gans pleaded that he was protecting his sight. "There's not a lot holding your eyeballs in your head," Ralph Citro, a modern-day cut man, said.

But the *New York Press* newspaper, which was not alone in its criticism, said Gans was "as yellow in heart as in his color." The *Press*, which played a part in coining the term "yellow journalism" to describe Joseph Pulitzer's *World* and William Randolph Hearst's *Journal*, said that Gans was "a man who quits on the slightest provocation. There is more of the coward in him than there is in all the other fighters in the ring put together."

Fights fixed by the fighters themselves were common a century ago, but Gans could have found easier ways to lose than he did to McFadden and Erne. Al Herford knew how to fix a fight, and he saw the best possibility toward the end of 1900. Chicago hoped to gain some of the attention New York was losing with the repeal of the Horton act, and even though only short fights, so-called exhibitions, were legal there, Chicago was turning out its share of boxers who attracted big crowds as police ignored the law. Gans would meet Terrible Terry McGovern, the featherweight champion, in a nontitle fight in Chicago on December 13. George Siler, who would referee, wrote in the *Chicago Daily Tribune* that the fight was "arousing more general interest than anything of the kind that has occurred in the Middle West for years." He called it "the most important" fight in Chicago's history.

Gans arrived by train on December 3, and the next day he began working out at bantamweight Harry Forbes's gym. For winning, he would collect the impressive sum of $8,000. Herford stood to keep most of it. But he had an idea how to make more.

Gans-McGovern was scheduled for just six rounds. Supposedly this meant that only sparring would be involved, no big punches would be thrown, and no one would get hurt. But Gans-McGovern was hardly an exhibition, and neither fighter thought of it as such, nor did the public. In the days after the fight was made, the betting was heavy—with the early money on Gans. The buildup was great, and everyone in Chicago knew that in this instance the word "exhibition" was meant to convey the opposite. Police prepared to wink at the Gans-McGovern match, and those officers on duty at the arena could enjoy themselves. The mayor, Carter Henry Harrison, Jr., endorsed the fight, despite the tension that usually accompanied a mixed-race bout.

Malachy Hogan, a Clark Street saloonkeeper and boxing referee, suggested in an article that he wrote for the *Chicago Times-Herald* that there could be disturbances between whites and blacks if Gans won. "If Terry should go down before the Baltimore lightweight," he wrote, "I make a guess that there will be a scene . . . Ninety-nine men in a hundred who follow the events of the ring would be sorely disappointed if the best little man ever produced should prove to have been overmatched against a boxer who has every advantage except the possible one of fighting pluck. Not that I predict a disorderly time, but McGovern's defeat would cause a big howl of disappointment from the thousands who have reached the conclusion that he is invincible."

McGovern was the greater attraction in the fight with Gans. *The Ring* magazine said that Johnstown, Pennsylvania, could claim two devastating forces: the flood of 1889 and Terrible Terry McGovern, who was born there. A redheaded Irishman, McGovern had grown up in Brooklyn as a street tough who gravitated to prizefights. He worked as a newsboy, earned a gold watch for winning an amateur boxing tournament, and turned pro at seventeen. He won the bantamweight championship by age nineteen and the featherweight championship two months before he turned twenty. His fame spread partly because his manager, Sam Harris, had invested in Broadway shows and had arranged for him to play the role of a boxer in a touring melodrama called *The Bowery After Dark.* McGovern's ring and stage earnings for 1900 were more than double the $50,000 annual salary of the president of the United States, William McKinley.

By December 1900, Gans was terrorizing opponents, determined to gain another title opportunity. He had scored nine knockouts since April. In his career he had won more than eighty fights and beaten men seventy pounds heavier. But for the McGovern fight, as he had against many white opponents, Gans agreed to terms that put him at a disadvantage. He would have to knock out McGovern to claim the winner's purse, whereas McGovern would be declared the winner simply by finishing on his feet. Gans considered the arrangement fair enough because McGovern had never fought backing up and would be within reach of a knockout punch.

Soon, however, the odds shifted dramatically in favor of McGovern. Late money on sports events usually is a sign people know that something significant has happened to one side or the other. It could be injury or illness. A fix could be in, and before the Chicago fight, there were rumors of a fix. The Gans side was suspected of arranging a McGovern victory.

Bookmakers found themselves overwhelmed with McGovern money. Some who continued to bet on Gans did so because they could not conceive of his losing to a featherweight, even the featherweight champion. Others considered it unthinkable that he would jeopardize his career by fixing a fight. In Baltimore, however, the unthinkable was happening. Blacks, having heard the rumors, were betting on McGovern.

Herford, trying to end speculation of a fix, made a show of betting $3,000 on Gans. But Gans had agreed to Herford's arrangement. Years later, he said he "expected to reap a harvest" from the fraud. Herford had promised him $40,000 to $45,000. Gans trained lightly. He jogged through the parks and streets of Chicago's South Side. He scarcely worked up a sweat in Forbes's gym.

The fight was set for Tattersall's, an arena at Dearborn and Sixteenth streets on the Near South Side that was named for the eighteenth-century London horse auction house. If it happened in boxing in Chicago, it happened at Tattersall's. The most impressive indoor sports arena in America west of the Stanford White–designed Madison Square Garden, Tattersall's was a plain, no-nonsense building of stone walls, brick parapets, and a high vaulted ceiling, its sheer bulk a perfect piece of the Chicago cityscape that took shape after the fire of 1871. Amos Alonzo Stagg's University of Chicago football teams occasionally played games there.

A Bob Fitzsimmons comeback fight at Tattersall's on October 28, 1899, against Geoffrey Thorne, the heavyweight champion of South Africa, brought out men in top hats, tails, and starched shirts, and a sprinkling of women in evening gowns. The writer Edgar Lee Masters, having obtained a free ringside ticket from Malachy Hogan, wrote in *Esquire* magazine: "You will find in the twenty-third book of the *Iliad* old Homer's description of the fight between the boxer Epeius and the boxer Euryalus, in which Epeius smote Euryalus, so that his legs sank beneath him . . . The Homeric fight reminds one of the contests of Fitz, for when he smote an antagonist the latter's 'glorious limbs' sank beneath him." And after Fitz smote Thorne in the first round, Masters added: "The blow was not over six inches in delivery—but what a sock! You could tell that from the way Thorne crumpled . . . They rubbed him with ammonia. They sprayed champagne upon him . . . It seemed to me several minutes before Thorne awoke to the realities."

Archrivals Tommy Ryan and Kid McCoy fought a six-round "exhibition" at Tattersall's, with Hogan as referee after he had downed several brandies at his bar beforehand. Hogan overlooked volleys of low blows by each fighter and, at the end of the brawl, declared McCoy the winner, whereupon Ryan punched Hogan on the chin. Hogan, a big man who served as his own bouncer, slugged it out with Ryan until police intervened.

The resourceful matchmaker Lou Houseman, who beneath his flat straw hat resembled Dr. No of the James Bond films, arranged to have the Gans-McGovern fight filmed to add to the sizable ticket revenue of close to $30,000 that the sellout crowd of about ten thousand would generate.

At seven o'clock on the evening of the fight, a boisterous crowd gathered for the weigh-in at Hogan's. McGovern weighed 124, but Gans failed by a pound and a quarter to make the 133-pound limit stipulated in the contract. Gans assured McGovern's manager Harris that he would hand over half his purse if he won. With that, the crowd shifted from Hogan's to the City Hotel bar on State Street, a respite from the cold on the way to Tattersall's and a place to bet on the fight. Most bet on McGovern.

At the arena, a man named Vernon Johns, who represented a

group of gamblers who had conspired with Herford, went up and down the aisles with a satchel around his neck looking for anyone who would bet on Gans. Johns acted confident that McGovern would win—he offered to wager any amount up to $20,000 on McGovern—and found takers eager to prove him wrong. Shortly, he returned with a better offer: He would bet up to $20,000 that McGovern would win by knockout. There were more takers. With a final proposition, he concentrated on the ringside seats: He would bet anyone that Gans would be stopped before the end of the fourth round. Many of the big shots in the expensive seats thought that idea preposterous, and they bet enough on Gans that Johns filled his satchel with bills.

Moments after the opening bell, the bettors realized they had been duped. As expected, McGovern waded in. Unexpectedly, Gans retreated from blows he normally would have blocked with ease. None of McGovern's punches looked threatening. Yet Gans stumbled backward toward the ropes. Toward the end of the round, Gans went down on his back from a left to the jaw. He got up at seven. But the hovering McGovern knocked him down again with a punch thrown just after the bell. Gans's seconds pulled him up and helped him to his corner. None, Herford included, protested the late punch.

The *Chicago Daily Tribune* reported that Gans "looked frightened as he came out of his corner" for round two. Within seconds, he was back on the canvas. And again. And again. And again. He kept falling down and getting up, as if he didn't know how to throw a fight—years later, he would say he wasn't very good at faking.

Backing away, he went down a sixth time.

The seventh time he stayed down.

He was balancing himself on his left knee when, at two minutes five seconds of the second round, he was counted out.

People booed. Some surged toward the ring, shouting "Lynch him!" and "Throw the faker into the lake!"

Police hurried both fighters down the aisles to their basement dressing rooms amid a shower of cigar butts and crumpled newspapers. Gans had to sneak out of the building. A riot was averted.

"If Gans was trying . . . I don't know much about the game," the referee and columnist Siler wrote in the next day's *Daily Tribune*. "The few blows he delivered were the weakest ever seen from a man of his known hitting abilities."

"I was unable to see where McGovern knocked Gans out," Siler also was quoted as saying. "I did notice, though, in the final fusillade of blows, that Gans went to the floor on the slightest pretext. The last blow struck was a glancing swing, partly on the side and partly on the top of Gans's head. For my part, I cannot see how such a blow could have put the man out. Gans, in my mind, never tried in the least."

One account said the bout was "heavily scented with crookedness." Another said that "one of the most gigantic gambling swindles ever planned was successfully carried out."

Chicago's City Council moved to enforce a law banning boxing, and Mayor Harrison, who had blessed the affair, concluded: "If the game is too bad for the council, it certainly is too bad for me."

Never in boxing has there been a fix of such consequence. The sport would not be legalized again in Chicago until 1926. And not another major fight would take place there until September 22, 1927, when Gene Tunney defeated Jack Dempsey with the help of the referee's "long count."

Gans made his situation worse by lying. He signed a statement for the *Chicago Times-Herald*: "The better man won. That is all I can give in explanation of the result. I did not lay down. I was hit hard early in the fight, and that seemed to take the wind out of me. I don't think there is anyone who can stand up before McGovern at the lightweight limit."

The day after his fix, Gans quietly left Chicago while Herford stayed behind to collect his money. Herford professed that Gans had done his best and claimed his fighter had told him between rounds that he was hurt by a punch, quoting him as saying: "I feel as I did when I was threatened with pneumonia."

Herford's payoff to Gans was somewhat less than the $40,000 to $45,000 promised. Gans ended up with $4,500.

Kid Parker, whom Gans had knocked out a month earlier, found it convenient to cancel a bout with him, saying nothing could be gained by fighting a faker.

The *Los Angeles Times* mocked him: "Joe Gans is said to be training hard for his next fight. Now, that is all superfluous, you know. It doesn't require any training to be able to tumble over and be counted out at the first punch."

A few days after the fight, Siler wrote in the *Daily Tribune* that Gans had "put a black mark against his record so wide and heavy he will never be able to erase it."

That was what Gans feared the most as his train rattled eastward through the night.

•

Two years later, after Gans had knocked out Frank Erne to win the lightweight title, Siler devoted a column in the *Daily Tribune* to the rise of black boxers. And, with an enlightened perspective, he called attention to boxing's oppressive power structure— principally, white managers' control over black boxers, which had never been more in evidence than in the fix at Tattersall's that he had refereed:

> Erne's defeat is to be deplored, not so much because he was beaten by a colored man and that colored man happened to be Joe Gans, as because Gans is under the management of Al Herford, to whom he is like clay in the hands of a potter.

Personally the new lightweight champion is a nice gentlemanly fellow but the man who coaches him to victory or defeat is one under suspicion by the boxing public. There is no denying the fact that Joe is a good fighter, probably the best in his class and under other management, despite his color, would be an honor to the profession. But now comes the question from critics, Will his manager, now that he is champion, permit him to fight to retain his title regardless of anything else, or will he bring him into more disrepute by compelling him to lose fights for the money that can be gained thereby?

Siler answered his own question. He predicted long reigns for Gans and the black welterweight champion, the Barbados-born Joe Walcott, the original Joe Walcott. He continued,

This does not speak well for the white pugilists, who outnumber their colored brethren at least twenty to one. But what can be done in the matter? If the whites cannot become proficient enough to beat the blacks, the latter must not only be tolerated but acknowledged the better men . . .

No one north of Mason and Dixon's line objects much to the colored fighter. Still, as a rule, they want to see him beaten when opposed to a white fighter. That is but natural. But why, if the ethics of the ring calls for fair play, should the colored fighter be roasted, hissed, hooted at, and otherwise harassed when contesting against a white? Why not take a dig at the white manager?

22

Go in," someone in Nelson's corner shouted as Nelson pursued Gans hard in the twenty-fourth round. The Associated Press already had given Nelson the twenty-third round, and now he fought as tenaciously as he ever had in his life. Responding to the cries of encouragement, he tried to finish Gans.

Nelson landed a hard left hand to the jaw, and Gans was forced to clinch. The AP reporter considered Nelson the winner of the twenty-fourth round. And Nelson continued his attack in the opening minute and a half of the twenty-fifth. The fight seemed to be slipping away from Gans.

But he battled back. The AP reported: "Joe awoke from his apparent somnolence and more than evened up matters."

In the second half of the twenty-fifth round, Gans looked like the fighter Bob Fitzsimmons described as "the cleverest fighter, big or little, that ever put on a glove," lavish praise in that Jim Corbett and Fitzsimmons himself were both cunning.

The twenty-sixth and twenty-seventh rounds also were close, but the pace of the fight slowed as Gans and Nelson wrestled with each other. It was past five o'clock. The sun had begun a descent that would take it behind Malapai Mountain. The temperature was dropping, but only slightly, into the nineties.

On the East Coast, it was dark, but people sought updates on the fight and the crowds on the streets grew. In New York, in the heavily black area centered around Amsterdam Avenue and Sixty-second Street, and for blocks to the west, cheering broke out each time someone shouted that Gans had done something well.

The outcome remained in doubt, although supposedly Homer had said "art obtains the prize," a credo that has endured in boxing with some notable exceptions, as in 1952 when Rocky Marciano, the slugger, caught up to the artful Jersey Joe Walcott and knocked him out. All else being fairly equal, smart fighters usually find a way to win. Sometimes they are able to psych out or outwit their foes during a fight. Sugar Ray Leonard demonstrated his snap-quick ability to recognize a critical moment halfway through the ninth round of a 1987 title fight with Marvin Hagler, coming off the ropes to seize Hagler's offensive out of necessity, because Leonard was trying to win a decision and felt if he lost the round he might lose the fight.

A timeline of outstanding thinkers in American sports could extend back from Tiger Woods—"I enjoy having to think my way around the golf course," he once said—to, say, Muhammad Ali and Arthur Ashe and Bill Bradley and Bill Russell and Ted Williams and Jackie Robinson and Gene Tunney and, drawn far enough, to Joe Gans.

"He was a brainy guy like Fitzsimmons," boxing historian Hank Kaplan said. "He was a thinking guy who punched when he had a clear opening, then hammered you with power."

He had been a thinker before he met Fitzsimmons; the ability had been instilled, perhaps, by his foster mother. Somehow he had it.

He was stoical, as Ashe would be; a student of his sport, like Bradley; as sworn to a scientific approach as Williams when he came up to bat; as calm as Tunney when Tunney rode in a little red Curtiss Oriole plane from his training camp in the Pocono Mountains to Philadelphia for his first fight with Dempsey in 1926—*The New York Times* said Tunney defied death—and gave the impression that the title fight that night was an afterthought.

Late in his career, April 1, 1908, when his brain was his best weapon, Gans found a way to beat a middling English lightweight named Spike Robson. Robson held both gloves in front of his face for protection, but he held them so close, only a few inches from his face, that Gans hit the back of Robson's left glove and drove it against his chin. Thus it was said that Gans caused an opponent to knock himself out.

"I hit his hand instead of waiting for an opening," Gans said. "It was very simple."

Before scouting became routine, Gans often would watch an upcoming opponent in action, sitting in the gallery reserved for blacks. He liked to take along a sparring partner, Harry Lenny, himself a student of boxing.

"We would sit in the gallery," Lenny said.

Sometimes we would watch only one round and then leave. Other times we might sit through two, three, even five rounds, before leaving. Gans would glue his eyes on the man in the ring and make mental notes. He might say to me, "Harry, notice how he tips his head to the right when he throws a left." I would nod. Or he would point out some other weakness that attracted his attention. But when Joe put on his hat and said, "Let's go, Harry," I knew he had seen enough and that he already knew exactly what he was going to do when he got that fellow into the ring.

Gans was never more prepared than for his second attempt at the lightweight championship against Frank Erne. In their first meeting in March 1900, before Gans had suffered the cut eye, Erne had been winning because Gans could not solve Erne's left hand. Erne had the ability to start his left as if it were a jab and, depending on his foe's reaction, continue with the jab or turn the punch into a hook. The punch with two options baffled most opponents. No one who sparred with Gans could imitate Erne's action except for Lenny, who would show Joe Louis before his rematch with Max Schmeling how to get away from the right hand Schmeling had used to win their first fight. Lenny suggested to Gans, "Why don't you drop your right over Erne's left?" Gans laughed and replied: "I'll get him in the first."

To counter Erne's left, Gans often shadowboxed in front of a mirror during the next two years. First he would play the part of Erne, then switch back to himself. One day, he showed Lenny the results. The two sparred, Lenny imitating Erne. Gans sent him sprawling with a right hand. Lenny could not have been happier to be knocked down.

On the night of May 12, 1902, Gans and Erne met at the International Athletic Club in Fort Erie, Ontario. They had to cross the border from Erne's hometown of Buffalo because of New York's ban on boxing, and thousands followed to witness the bout. In the first round, Gans knocked out Erne and became the first American-born black champion.

"I learned that he always dropped his left before he jabbed or hooked," Gans said. "And another thing, I learned that when he gave ground, he only went back six or eight inches instead of a full step or two. I planned it out. I would feint him to draw the hook or jab, and when he dropped the left or stepped back, I would shoot my own right over. What he did was step back and, since I knew exactly how far back he'd go, I just aimed to the spot. He bobbed right into the punch."

On January 19, 1906, when Gans knocked out Mike Sullivan in San Francisco to win the welterweight title—the first fight Gans arranged as his own manager—George Blake, a corner man for Packey McFarland and an acquaintance of Gans's, watched.

"As the fight progressed," Blake said, "one of Joe's hooks caught Mike beneath the ear, and Mike winced. It wasn't long after that when Mike was nailed under the ear again. The blow did not seem very hard, but it did the trick. I was very impressed with the way his brain worked. One day he said to me, 'If you happen to hit a man in a certain place that hurts, that is the place to hit him again. You only have to hit him half as hard there as any other place to finish him.'"

Time and distance, Gans often said, were "the two most important words in my business." He had the patience to wait for an opening—he didn't knock out Sullivan until the fifteenth round of their scheduled twenty-rounder. And by the time he had the opening, he knew exactly the distance his punch should travel. He had measured it in his mind.

If he could get away with it, he would actually take the measure of an opponent by extending one arm or the other until it almost touched him. This tactic would become routine in boxing, especially if an opponent was in no shape to avoid being measured for a knockout punch. Sam Langford, the greatest boxer never to fight for a title because he was black, learned how to measure an opponent by watching Gans stick out his right hand during a fight and hold it there without attempting a punch.

"I asked him why," Langford said. "'I wanted to measure the distance and see how far I'd have to reach to knock him out,' said Joe. And sure enough, in the middle of the [next] round Joe flattened his man . . . His act of measuring distance was new to me but it worked almost to the letter."

•

Gans had an advantage over Langford and other black fighters of the era: Gans received more support in the press, both from predominantly black newspapers and white ones, from papers across the country and hometown ones. Ironically, a likely source of acclaim, the black press of Gans's home city, failed to perceive—at least initially—his intelligent approach to boxing. Baltimore's weekly *The Afro-American Ledger* was antiboxing and, like other publications and many people, did not yet realize the impact athletes could have on society.

In 1902, the year Gans became champion, *The Afro-American Ledger* complained in an editorial that Gans received "more space in the white papers than all the respectable colored people in the state" and wondered why "illiterate prizefighters should be more influential role models than respectable colored people such as Booker T. Washington and W.E.B. Du Bois." The newspaper concluded that the best way for a black man to break into print in the white press was to "become a fighter or a criminal."

A few years later, the newspaper's editors changed their minds. They praised Gans's excellence as a boxer. And an editorial criticizing a Southern white man who had said that "the Negro is 'inaccessible to ideas'" hailed Gans, among others, as "a man of 'ideas.'"

Langford and Gans belonged to different weight classes and did not feel the need to outdo each other even though they fought once, the heavier Langford winning a close decision in a fifteen-round nontitle bout in Boston's Criterion Club in 1903. In more than sixty fights over five years, the loss to Langford and a decision favoring Jack Blackburn after six rounds were Gans's only defeats.

Gans never offered an excuse for tiring in the late rounds against Langford, but on the previous night, Gans had also fought—and in Philadelphia. He had beaten Dave Holly, then stayed up all night playing cards on the train to Boston.

"Nobody can keep you from being a champion," Gans told Langford enthusiastically when they met up in a nightclub after their fight—forgetting, momentarily, that Jim Crow was their toughest foe.

Langford happily accepted Gans's offer of boxing tips, and they would meet again for pedagogic purposes. But Langford encountered racial barriers that may have cost him as many as three titles. To remain in prizefighting, he was forced to fight other black boxers, such as Harry Wills, whom he fought at least seventeen times. "In those days the people who ran the fights didn't want white guys to fight colored guys," Jack Dempsey told the writer Jimmy Cannon. "Sam probably would have knocked me out."

Late in his career, Langford fought blind in one eye, and by the time his career ended in 1926, he had lost most of his vision. He lived on until 1956, more than enough time for him to see, however hazily, Joe Louis.

"He can hit, he is fast and is no slouch at employing ring craft," Langford said after a Louis training session. "He is the marvel of the age. I consider him another Gans."

•

A thinker like Joe Gans, little George Dixon came as close to being self-taught as any athlete. But he, too, had a mentor.

Like Langford, Dixon was born and grew up in Halifax, Nova Scotia. As a schoolboy in the 1880s, he often visited a man named Bailey, who got the newspapers from the United States. The night boat from Boston carried copies of that city's papers, and largely from those sports pages Bailey formed his ideas about boxing. Dixon would sit and listen to Bailey's stories of fights and fighters, and Bailey's opinions about how to box— simply winding up and trying to slug the other guy wasn't it. Bailey concluded instead that a boxer was apt to find success with a more scientific approach—radical thinking for the time. Dixon would then box imaginary opponents in a manner based only on Bailey's skimpy information.

Like Gans, who was called on to fight the street tough outside the Baltimore fish market, Dixon, fifteen years old and weighing about seventy-five pounds, had to please his friends by fighting the local bully, a bigger kid named Johnson. They battled with bare knuckles in a barn, with Dixon apparently winning in three rounds—either someone declared him the winner or Johnson quit.

But Dixon went home with both eyes swollen almost shut, and his mother whipped him until he promised that he would not fight again. Soon after, however, she died, and in September 1887 Dixon's father gathered the children and immigrated to Boston, just as Langford would. Dixon frequented the city's fight clubs, watching, boxing, improving. Tom O'Rourke, both a manager and a promoter as Al Herford would be, latched onto him.

The blustery O'Rourke was another example of a self-serving white man who wielded power in the sport. And Dixon, as would Gans, found it difficult to free himself from a white boss.

In 1892, Dixon fought an exhibition with Jim Watson of Paterson, New Jersey. O'Rourke was interested in Watson, thinking that as a promising white boxer he might develop into a drawing card. "Don't hit this fellow hard, Georgie," O'Rourke told Dixon. "He is only an amateur, and I don't want him hurt."

Dixon went easy on Watson. But late in the second round, Watson, his confidence growing, began fighting as hard as he could. And he kept up the assault. In the third round, Dixon surprised Watson—and O'Rourke—with a powerful combination: a left to Watson's midsection, a right uppercut, and a left to the jaw. Watson fell flat, and the fight was stopped.

O'Rourke, a big man who had fought as a heavyweight, lost his temper. *The Boston Daily Globe* reported that he approached Dixon and "struck him a hard blow on the chin."

"You're too fresh, Georgie," the newspaper quoted O'Rourke, "and you can take that for your smart trick."

Dixon didn't fight O'Rourke, but said he intended to get a new manager who wouldn't make a "punching bag" of him. But he didn't. O'Rourke had influence in boxing, and Dixon, perhaps, realized he could not hire anyone with better connections. Or maybe it was that Dixon already was attracted to O'Rourke's sister, whom he eventually married. In any event, he reconciled himself to taking O'Rourke's abuse. And his career flourished. He became renowned as "Little Chocolate"—white sportswriters gave no thought to tagging black boxers with nicknames that identified them by race; Langford was the "Boston Tar Baby," and, even three decades later, Joe Louis "the Brown Bomber." White boxers tended to be nicknamed after their birthplace: Rocky Marciano, "the Brockton Blockbuster"; Jake La Motta, "the Bronx Bull"; Tony Zale, born in Gary, Indiana, "the Man of Steel."

On June 27, 1892, Dixon won the featherweight championship—making him the first black to win a world title—by knocking out Fred Johnson at Coney Island. In 1894, Dixon watched a plainly inventive Gans employ poetic skills to win a bout at the Avon Club in Baltimore. "Why, there is the making of a high-class fighter, if he will only take care of himself and work," Dixon told reporters.

Frequently, there was talk that Gans and Dixon would make a good match and that they would draw a big crowd in New York even though both were black. But O'Rourke did not want Dixon to fight Gans, so he didn't, but O'Rourke needn't have worried. The bigger and younger Gans had too much respect for Dixon to fight him.

O'Rourke, who later promoted fights in New York, was a friend of Max Schmeling and went to wish him well in his dressing room at Yankee Stadium before his first fight with Joe Louis.

"My dying wish would be that you defeat this Louis," O'Rourke told Schmeling.

On the way out of the room, O'Rourke was stricken by a heart attack and died.

Dixon was Gans's best man at his wedding in New York.

•

In the twenty-eighth round at Goldfield, Gans hit Nelson three times in the head, knocking him halfway across the ring. The bell likely saved Nelson again, as it had at the end of the twentieth round.

In New York City, people kept Broadway jammed as they read the bulletins. At San Francisco's Presidio Hospital, patients skipped dinner to stay close to the special telegraph line routed into their common room.

Gans's effectiveness so late in the fight surprised no one more than Al Herford. Back in Baltimore, he had predicted that Gans would lose if the fight went beyond fifteen rounds. But Gans had more endurance than Herford thought.

In the twenty-ninth round, the Associated Press said he "peppered" Nelson "mercilessly." But as it had in the early rounds, the AP offered a countervailing observation: "Nelson's recuperative powers are almost superhuman."

In the thirtieth round, Gans continued his offensive. The only serious blow by Nelson, other than a head butt, was an apparently deliberate punch after the bell. Fans jumped to their feet and booed him, and someone called for three cheers for Gans—and the crowd responded, making for a rare scene in America, a predominantly white crowd cheering for a black man.

In the thirty-first round Gans and Nelson barely moved. In the thirty-second, Gans shot lefts and rights that found their mark: Nelson's left eye was almost closed. Nelson spent much of the round with his head lowered, propelling himself like a missile, mostly missing Gans, ignoring Siler's pleas. Nelson seemed disoriented; the bell may have saved him again.

What followed was one of the most remarkable rounds in boxing history. In the thirty-third round, Gans came on strong. The AP reported him beating Nelson's face to "jelly." He closed

Nelson's left eye even more. "Nelson bled profusely," the AP said. "It was a sight to behold."

Gans seemed on the verge of winning the fight. But then, inexplicably, something happened. He stopped fighting. He stopped entirely. Could this be how the long afternoon was going to end? He seemed to have injured his left leg, or foot. He stood on his right foot and shook the other. It was a crazy sight as he hopped about. Did he have a cramp? Did he pull a muscle?

Whatever the case, Nelson was too weak to capitalize. He was half-blind. Gans clinched, and the round ended.

He was in trouble, but he had camouflaged his injury because he did not want Nelson to know where he had been hurt. When he hit Nelson's head he had broken a bone in his right hand. Had he had the wrappings under his gloves, the bone might not have broken.

Now he had only one good fist—his left. But he was too smart to let Nelson know that. So he limped to his corner instead, and had one of his seconds rub his leg.

When he learned of Gans's deception, Tex Rickard said: "It was one of the craftiest things I ever saw a man do in the heat of the battling, a thing which thoroughly attested to Joe's great ring generalship."

Gans working out (San Francisco History Center, San Francisco Public Library)

Gans with a group in San Rafael, California, before a fight in San Francisco in 1904. Al Herford, Gans's manager at the time, is seated at the right in the photo, wearing a hat. (Courtesy of Anne T. Kent California Room, Marin County Free Library)

Goldfield, 1906 (The Gary Schultz Collection)

Tex Rickard, promoter of the Gans-Nelson fight in Goldfield, with $30,000 of purse money in stacks of gold coins (The Gary Schultz Collection)

Gans and adviser Larry Sullivan confer in Goldfield. (The Gary Schultz Collection)

Battling Nelson making a fist, with his manager, Billy Nolan, to his right, and promoter Tex Rickard. In the background, the Goldfield fight arena is being built. (The Gary Schultz Collection)

Gans at the scale used for the fight's three weigh-ins; Nelson is at the left
(The Gary Schultz Collection)

Gans, seated in a corner of the ring before the fight, holding an umbrella
to shield himself from the sun on September 3, 1906 (The Gary Schultz Collection)

The two fighters pose for their gloved handshake. (Nevada Historical Society)

Fight action in which Gans is trying to help Nelson to his feet (The Gary Schultz Collection)

In his second fight against Nelson, on July 4, 1908, at Colma, California, Gans is down as referee Jack Welch counts. (Cayton Sports, Inc.)

In the fourteenth round of their second fight, Gans rallies and connects with a left to Nelson's head. But Nelson wins by knockout in the seventeenth round. (Cayton Sports, Inc.)

In their third and final fight, on September 9, 1908, again at Colma, Gans fails to rise in the twenty-first round and is counted out by referee Eddie Smith.

(Cayton Sports, Inc.)

Near death from tuberculosis and en route from Arizona to Baltimore in 1910, Gans is carried on a stretcher in Chicago. (© Chicago History Museum)

James Jackson, bartender for Gans, taking a last look at what remained of Gans's Goldfield Hotel in Baltimore, which became a grocery store before it was torn down in 1960 (Photograph by Ralph Dohme, © The Baltimore Sun)

23

Gans decided that his best chance to beat Nelson was by battering his right eye until it closed. Having almost closed Nelson's left eye and bruised and cut him around the right eye, Gans planned to jab at the right eye until he lowered it like a shade. That would force Siler to stop the fight if, in the process, Gans didn't knock out Nelson. As it was, Nelson was fighting partially blind, and even fighters with two good eyes sometimes don't know a punch has been thrown until it hits them. When fighters say they didn't see a punch coming, they almost always mean it literally.

But if Nelson could see out of only one eye, Gans would be fighting with only one hand. His right-hand punches would be little more than distractions. He had lost any chance to knock out Nelson with one hard right. The spectators, who thought something was the matter with his leg, wondered if he even would come out for the thirty-fourth round.

By then they had grown restless. They were jammed together, they were hot, they were tired, they were hungry. Some bought sandwiches. A miner in the audience bellowed: "This is a union camp. You can't fight over eight hours."

For the next six rounds—from the thirty-fourth through the thirty-ninth—Gans and Nelson leaned on each other, and each grabbed and held. Between rounds, Gans vomited over the ropes.

Nelson continued to butt and persisted in resting his head on one of Gans's shoulders. Gans protested twice to Siler. By now, Siler had had at least a dozen chances to disqualify Nelson. Again he opted to let the fight continue. Jack London had written of Nelson that "the abysmal brute in him gives him a tremendous capacity to move and to keep on moving . . . ceaselessly moving." But the AP reported that both Gans and Nelson now "tottered around" the ring.

During the thirty-fifth round, the sun seemed almost to touch Malapai Mountain and shadows spread across the desert floor. September's late light brought the question: Which would come first, the end of the fight, or darkness?

The AP said that at the end of the thirty-ninth round, Nelson's left eye was closed. He had not won a round since the twenty-fourth, although some rounds had been essentially even. Gans used the fortieth round to flick his left hand repeatedly into Nelson's right eye. He closed it halfway. At the beginning of the forty-first round, he shouted facetiously to Nelson's manager Nolan, "What time is it?"

At the end of the forty-first, both fighters staggered to their corners. As Gans sat on his stool, it seemed he might not get back to his feet. Nelson, too. And Nelson's face looked like freshly ground beef.

Somehow, both answered the bell for the forty-second round.

Gans opened with a straight left to his foe's misshapen face. The two clinched. Nelson positioned his head on Gans's shoulder. Having dropped his right arm to his side, Nelson swung it upward twice. Both punches landed below Gans's waistband. Next, he drew back his left arm and hit Gans yet another low blow, this one even lower than the others, harder than the others. It was Nelson's left half-scissors hook—but it was delivered too low. It caught Gans in the groin. Gans, the AP said, "slowly sank to the floor."

He went down in sections, like an imploding building. His

left knee touched first, his right knee next. He tumbled forward, onto his right side. Finally, he stretched full length on his back.

Nelson stood over him momentarily, but Siler pushed him toward his corner. The referee starting counting as he stepped toward Gans, then leaned over him. Nolan, attempting to influence Siler into thinking that Gans had quit, shouted, "You've won, Bat, you've won."

With that, Siler waved his arms. Indeed, the fight was over. But the winner was on the floor. Siler disqualified Nelson for the last low blow. The referee helped Gans up and raised his arm in victory.

There was cheering—for Gans and, as the fans were sunbaked and weary, for the end of the fight. No one outside Nelson's corner objected to the outcome.

The fight had taken two hours and forty-eight minutes, the longest championship fight of the twentieth century. It ended at 6:11 p.m., in the shadows.

The AP reported: "The blow was clearly observed by everyone in the arena and there was not a murmur of dissent from the spectators as the long-drawn-out battle was terminated."

The *Los Angeles Herald*'s writer noted that the foul was "so obvious that not even men who had bet on Nelson could say that it had not been committed."

"It was as clear a foul as I ever saw," Siler said, "and I could do nothing except disqualify Nelson. It was my only possible course."

People cheered Siler.

They cheered Gans.

They hissed and booed Nelson. Sheriff's deputies surrounded him, protecting him from those he had angered with his fouls and those who had bet on him and lost.

•

Gans had done the inconceivable. Despite his race, he had gained all the recognition in the world a man could want, surely as much as a black man in America could have. In advance he fulfilled Picasso's concept of an artist: "You must do what is not there, what has never been done."

Two telegrams.

Having rested behind the stands, Gans wanted first to respond to his foster mother's message to him before the fight to "bring back the bacon." He dictated his reply to her: YOUR BOY JOE IS BRINGING THE BACON AND LOTS OF GRAVY.

A few hours later, someone at the Merchants Hotel wanted to send a telegram and asked for a messenger. A teenager named Jim Casey pedaled his bicycle out to the hotel and knocked on the guest's door. When it opened, he came face-to-face with Joe Gans himself.

"Here, kid," Gans said, "have this message sent by telegraph."

Casey, who eventually would cofound the United Parcel Service, fled Goldfield just a few weeks later after one of his coworkers bumped into a craps dealer with his bike and was shot dead. Casey wished he had kept Gans's note and recalled to whom it was sent. But he remembered what it said: THE DOG QUIT IN THE 42ND ROUND.

•

That night, there was trouble in America.

Gans's victory "caused the first serious outbreaks of racial violence against blacks as a result of a boxing match," Arthur Ashe wrote in *A Hard Road to Glory: A History of the African-American Athlete 1619–1918*. "Police reported incidents across the country attributed to the bout. William Conway, a black bar patron in Flushing, New York, had his skull fractured by three white customers. Anthony Roberts, a black doorman at the St. Urban Apartments on New York City's Central Park West, told police he fought off two white attackers with a razor and a small pistol."

In Chicago, the AP reported violence from "race excitement" as word of the result spread. Several whites chased a black man through the streets and attacked him after he fell from exhaustion on the steps of the home where he worked. "One thousand men and women, black and white, joined in a race riot tonight in South Chicago near Hegewisch, the home of Battling Nelson, as a result of the downfall of the pugilistic idol of the whites, and for half an hour fought a pitched battle in the streets with fists, clubs, and stones. Forty policemen used their clubs freely before the hostilities were brought to check." Four men were hospitalized and hundreds suffered minor injuries. Forty-two were arrested.

In Hegewisch, Nelson's mother told a reporter: "I can scarcely realize that my son, after so many victories, has been defeated, and by a colored man."

In Dallas, police jailed several black men for no other reason than their glee over Gans's victory.

The Atlanta newspapers played up the Chicago and Dallas disturbances, emphasizing that interracial boxing threatened the "Southern way of life." *The Atlanta Constitution* ran a front-page story under the headline RACE WAR IS PROVOKED BY GANS-NELSON FIGHT. *The Atlanta Journal* claimed that Gans's victory stirred up "rough elements of negroes in Dallas."

Racial tension in Atlanta boiled over before the month was out. From September 22 to 26, whites staged a sustained attack on blacks in what came to be known as the Atlanta Race Riot of 1906. At least twenty-six people were killed. All except two were black.

24

The next day's newspapers stripped banner headlines above their accounts of Gans's victory: GOLDFIELD WITNESSES TERRIFIC RING BATTLE . . . GANS WINS ON A FOUL AFTER WHIPPING NELSON ON MERITS . . . GANS RETAINS TITLE AND GIVES WORLD ITS GREATEST FIGHT.

Most of the stories ran on page one or on the fronts of sports sections. The majority opinion was that Nelson should have been disqualified earlier than he had been. Siler said that for the sake of the paying customers he wanted the fighters to decide the ending, but that in the end he had no choice. "Every man in the arena saw that I overlooked many fouls on which I would have plenty of excuse to have stopped the fight with a decision for Gans," he said.

Siler's paper, the *Chicago Daily Tribune*, even referred to Gans as a "hero."

R. A. Smyth of *The San Francisco Call* described the fight as "one of the most desperate engagements in the history of the ring." He said that Nelson's blood "took on a deep crimson in the garish light," and that "his work showed an utter absence of science." Gans, meanwhile, was "the Paderewski of the boxing glove."

Edward Clarke, in a page one piece for *The Call*, said the fight was too gory for "some hundreds of women and a few children who were—the latter for the first time in ring history—

admitted to an arena where only men should have been. It is a men's game."

A young prospector named Fred Sander described the fight as ghastly in a letter to his future wife, Charity, who was visiting in Wyoming: "I believe Nelson can stand more punishment than any man in the world . . . It was really too brutal to look at. I was glad it ended when it did, and the way it did, as they were both pretty badly beaten up."

Even after his most celebrated victory, Gans was reminded that his skin color placed him among the most oppressed people in America. Newspapers casually stereotyped him. The *San Francisco Chronicle* said he was "so well muscled that he resembles a carving of the perfect man in ebony." Other newspapers referred to him, in typical language, as a "nigger" or a "coon."

The Salt Lake Herald published an unsigned poem based on "Casey at the Bat":

> *In Franklin Lane, and Darktown, too, the sun is shining*
>   *bright;*
> *The Coons are laughing loudly and talking 'bout the*
>   *fight;*
> *They're eating big and drinking deep—Oh, hear the*
>   *darkies shout!*
> *But there is no joy for white men—Battling Nelson's*
>   *down and out!*

A few days later, the same Salt Lake paper ran a cartoon meant to show humorously the predicament of white fighters who had drawn the color line, but it depicted more vividly the reality that African Americans faced. The cartoonist drew Gans as a Sambo figure and depicted his speech in a racist patois: "Tell the gemmen ah' have decided to draw the color line!" In the drawing, white title contenders hoping to fight the black champion try to camouflage their color. Jimmy Britt blackens his face, saying, "I wonder if my complexion is on straight." Already in blackface, Nelson declares himself to be "Right from sunny Africa!"

Harry C. Carr of the *Los Angeles Times* held his own as an apologist for the white man, and Nelson specifically. He quoted Nelson as saying that he was on the verge of victory except that "Gans kept running his old wiry wool in my face until he made it as raw as beefsteak."

It's questionable whether Carr spoke to Nelson, who went into seclusion after the fight. Carr claimed to have seen Nelson in his hotel room, or at least he saw "one belligerent eye peeking out of a swath of bandages."

As for a quote he attributed to Gans, Carr may have made it up. He used a dialect he probably thought would sound like a black man, and he has Gans praising Nelson: "'Yas sar,' said Joe, 'I feel as good as any one could after fo'ty-two rounds like 'hat. Yas sar, it was rough fighting, but you must give it to Bat that he was game.'"

A rumor spread that Nelson was dangerously ill and likely to die as a result of the beating he had taken. The truth was bad enough: He was confined to his hotel room, and two doctors ordered him to bed while they cared for him. They warned of dire consequences if he attempted a long trip immediately.

The Hearst syndicate's Bill Naughton reported that Nelson had suffered "hemorrhages of the head and bowels," that he had been "in a very precarious condition following the beating," but that "now the physicians in attendance believe that all danger is passed."

Rickard sent an associate to visit Nelson and determine his condition, and the man reported back that Nelson's face was "cut and swollen into a shapeless mass," but that he would recover.

•

That afternoon, Sullivan drove Gans from his hotel to town. Miners, pleased with the fight's outcome, chased after the car. Gans looked as if he had been in a fight—his eyes and cheekbones were slightly swollen, as was the back of his right hand where the bone had been broken. But he didn't look like a prizefighter who had fought forty-two rounds against the most vicious opponent in the sport.

In town, a gleeful mob surrounded his car. Gans made several short speeches, either standing in the car or alongside it. He thanked people for their hospitality, and he promised to fight anyone they demanded.

Entering an ice cream parlor, he came upon Billy Nolan seated at the counter. Nolan had the temerity to say to Gans: "I have no hard feelings. Come on and have something." Gans laughed and ordered a soda, and he invited everyone in the place to have one on him.

A few minutes later, Siler walked in and saw Nolan. They didn't speak. Nolan had been accusing Siler of harassing Nelson during the fight and went so far as to claim that gamblers intended to pay off the referee for awarding the fight to Gans. For that allegation, Siler sued Nolan for $50,000, but he later dropped the case after Nolan apologized.

To reporters, Gans offered details of Nelson's behavior as the forty-two rounds unfolded. By Gans's account, Nelson treated him worse than Mike Leonard did. "Every minute of the fight he cursed and insulted me, spitting in my face and calling me every foul name he could lay his tongue to. But he could not provoke me into losing my temper."

Gans said he had been offered $25,000 to let Nelson win, affirming prefight rumors of a fix. Eddie Graney of San Francisco—he was known as "Tuxedo Eddie" for the formal attire he wore when he refereed—explained that several men from the West Coast proposed the deal, and that at least one acquaintance of Gans advised him to take the money and then double-cross them. Graney said he warned Gans that his safety could be threatened if he agreed to a fix, and that he surely would be in danger if he double-crossed the fixers. Graney said he counseled Gans to reject the proposed fix because it could be a trick in which Nolan might be tipped off, letting Nelson avoid the fight that Gans needed badly for the money, and for the satisfaction.

A few stories, however, contended that Gans tricked Siler into calling a halt, but they are all questionable.

George Graham Rice, Goldfield's mining stock manipulator, offered the most detailed version in his autobiography, *My Adventures with Your Money*:

> The fight had progressed for twenty rounds or more, when I began to doubt the ability of Gans to win . . . I hailed Mr. Sullivan at the ringside.
>
> "This doesn't look like the cinch for Gans you said it would be," I whispered.
>
> "Wait a minute," Mr. Sullivan replied, "I'll go to Gans's corner . . . and find out . . ." Mr. Sullivan went over to Gans's corner and came back. "Gans says he can't win this fight, but he won't lose . . ."
>
> The fight had continued through the fortieth round, when Mr. Sullivan again repaired to Gans's corner and held another animated whispered conversation with him.
>
> In the forty-second round Gans all of a sudden went down, rolled over and, holding his hand under his belt, let out a yell of anguish that indicated to the excited multitude that Nelson had fouled him frightfully.
>
> In another instant Mr. Sullivan had clambered to the ring. Confusion reigned. The audience was on its feet. Pushing his fist into the referee's face, Mr. Sullivan cried: "Now, Siler, you saw that foul, didn't you? It's a foul, isn't it? Gans wins, doesn't he?"

All of this happened quick as a flash. Mr. Siler, pale as a ghost, whispered something inaudibly.

Mr. Sullivan, turning to the assemblage and raising both arms to the skies, yelled: "Gentlemen, the referee declares Gans the winner on a foul!"

The audience acclaimed his decision with salvos of applause.

Egregiously, Bob Edgren, a sports columnist for New York's *The World*, turned over much of his column a few days after the fight to a letter writer, a common practice by columnists trying to fill their space. Edgren did not even identify the person, but called him "a sporting friend" who had attended the fight, and then let his "friend" claim that the low blow "didn't hurt Gans at all," that he had "played one of his old foxy tricks and got away with it."

Years later, *The Chicago Defender* published the recollections of an Ernest Summerall, who supposedly claimed before he died that Gans said he had told his corner men that he intended to drop from a low blow and that he would stay down if Siler did not begin counting, but would get up immediately if Siler began counting. As it happened, Siler did begin counting, and by the time he'd reached "four" and called off the fight, Gans still had not gotten up.

The consensus among reporters at ringside was that by the forty-second round both fighters were weak, but that Gans was on the verge of closing Nelson's right eye, which would have ended the fight. Or, had the two still been on their feet at the onset of darkness, Siler likely would have declared Gans the winner—it no longer was the practice to resume the next day, as had been the case with many protracted bare knuckle fights. It was unlikely, the reporters believed, that Siler would have ruled a draw, given his reputation for honesty and Nelson's antics throughout the fight. As Siler said later: "Gans, without the foul, was clearly entitled to the decision."

The New York *World's* Barton W. Currie, the only New York writer to cover the fight, emphasized that Gans had dominated Nelson and earned the victory, and that Nelson's tactics warranted an earlier disqualification and that he had angered the fans: "There are several thousand pretty tough citizens of Goldfield who would like to escort him out of town on a rail or, following a custom of the desert, stake him out on the alkali with a rattlesnake for an interesting companion."

Thomas Aloysius Dorgan of the *New York Journal* wrote: "Will there ever be another man like Joe Gans? . . . What is the use of any man trying to beat Gans now. There is no way to beat him."

•

Two days after the fight, Gans and "Mrs. Gans" received a rousing send-off at the Goldfield depot. At Reno, from the steps of a Pullman car, he greeted yet another crowd when his train stopped there. "I had Nelson beaten and was letting him wear himself out before I attempted to put him to the floor for good," he said.

The next day, Nelson left Goldfield quietly, "without any blare of trumpets," according to the *Los Angeles Herald*. A young attorney named George Springmeyer who happened to be riding the same train was "shocked" by Nelson's appearance. As Springmeyer told it, Nelson's "head appeared to have swollen to twice its normal size, and the bruised flesh had cracked and turned violent hues of green, yellow, and purple . . ."

A few days later, Nelson wrote a letter from a train bound for Illinois to the city editor of *The Goldfield Daily Sun* in which he called Gans a "dirty cur of a skunk."

"I don't like a nigger no how," he wrote in the letter. "The time I kicked him I am sorry I didn't kill him as any man that attempts to call my mother vile names, especially a nigger, ought to be killed."

As for himself, he was doing fine, he added in a postscript: He was about to open a ten-week engagement at a theater in Chicago.

Rickard announced a paid attendance of 6,972—the total attendance was 7,491—and ticket sales of $69,715. Rickard's profit of $13,215 was less than Nelson's and even less than what Gans made after collecting his bets. It was enough, however, to keep Rickard interested in promoting prizefights even though, years later, he admitted to betting heavily on Nelson.

From that start in a distant place, Rickard went to New York, where he worked his charms equally well with cigar-stub-chewing roughnecks in overheated gyms and the well-to-do on the Upper East Side. If he could make it in Goldfield, he could make it anywhere.

He would change the sport. Because once he latched onto Jack Dempsey, Rickard took boxing into a time when it became a big stadium event, and after his death a more profitable enterprise yet with live showings of bouts in theaters and large halls on closed-circuit TV, and still later an even bigger business with pay per view and corporate sponsorships.

"I never knew what the fight game offered until then," Rickard said years later. "I wasn't a boxing expert but what happened in the Gans-Nelson show made me think."

•

For a while, Goldfield continued to prosper. There was a nervous time in December 1907, when violence between union workers and mine owners threatened to erupt and Roosevelt sent in about three hundred federal troops to satisfy a worried Governor Sparks. In the national consciousness, however, Goldfield had peaked with the Gans-Nelson fight. The town's slow decline began two years later, as mining profits diminished, and in 1923 a fire, which started with an explosion in a bootlegger's still, burned down much of the town. By then, almost all of the $86 million in gold that the camp produced had been taken from the ground, and the place turned back into a desert wilderness, becoming as empty as Parmeter Kent foresaw in the very first edition of his *Goldfield Gossip* in 1906.

"It is a pitiful thing, and a melancholy," he wrote, "that of all these mills and houses and people and mines which are today Goldfield's, there shall not remain in fifty years more than a heap of scrap-iron, a few cans half-buried in the drifting sands, and an odd rib-bone to tell the story of man's earlier habitation of this spot. Fifty years is long life for a mining town. There is no respite from the certain decay that must fall upon it; no alternative. It is enough to make angels weep."

PART TWO

It always amazes me how easily men of the highest talents and eminence can be forgotten in this careless world—for example, the incomparable Joe Gans, lightweight champion of the world in the days when I was young.

—H. L. Mencken, "Master of Gladiators,"
The New Yorker, *April 25, 1942*

25

Knowing when to quit has eluded most great athletes. Bill Russell knew when. So did Jim Brown and Barry Sanders. Boxing had its Tunney and Marciano. But with the end of a career at hand, most of the best athletes fail to resist the temptation to go on.

Most of the exceptional ones continue, perhaps because they want to exhaust all their talents. Not unlike heads of corporations, politicians, climbers of every sort, they may see signs they should stop, but they ignore them. Great athletes—and boxers are as good an example as any—spend everything they have in performing, more often than not because the sport is what they are; it's a kind of death when they leave.

We everyday people say, *Quit while you're ahead.* And when they do, we applaud. We may miss them, but we are spared watching their diminishment. For many boxers, however, shifting to a new pursuit too often signals weakness, a giving up. There are many more Evander Holyfields than Marcianos. Because to stop is so very hard.

Consider the night of June 17, 2000, at the Staples Center in Los Angeles when Shane Mosley beat Oscar de la Hoya for the welterweight championship. It wasn't the fight. It was what happened beforehand. Sitting close to the ring, one could hear a distant cheering somewhere near the back of the arena. The cheering grew louder and louder, and it came forward like an ocean wave until it became an irresistible roar. If you had ever known that kind of cheering, you'd never want to give it up. Muhammad Ali took his seat.

26

Even in the prize ring we have our Joe Gans," Bishop Alexander Walters, president of the National Afro-American Council, the first nationwide civil rights organization in the United States, proclaimed in an October 1906 speech in New York as he demanded equal rights for African Americans. The reference to Gans drew cheers and rousing applause.

The victory over Battling Nelson brought Gans more attention than his having been the lightweight champion for four years, and a dominant fighter before that. Beating Nelson made Gans prominent in a way no other black athlete had been.

Money followed the fame. White fighters suddenly realized that a black man could make them a good payday, and they lined up to take him on. Promoters vied to gain his attention. Vaudeville operators made him thousand-dollar-a-week offers. Newspaper editorial page writers, who had ignored not only black boxers but virtually the entire black American experience, gave space to Gans. Rex Beach, a bestselling author and colleague of Jack London, would search him out for a magazine profile, a form of journalism that was just coming into vogue.

The Goldfield Daily Sun declared that Gans had done more for blacks in one day than Booker T. Washington had in his entire life, an overstatement born of the mining camp's postfight euphoria. *The Salt Lake Herald* pounced on the Goldfield paper's claim: "It is our honest opinion that Gans' victory over

Nelson has done real harm to the colored race. It has given many of its members the idea that the black is the physical, if not the mental and social superior of the white. The dispatches since the fight have told of numerous encounters between negroes and whites as a result of it."

Gans's defeat of Nelson prompted some newspapermen to tone down their racist rhetoric, but an undercurrent of bias, to say the least, remained. "Whether one likes it or not," W. D. Rishel wrote in *The Salt Lake Herald*, "you have to hand it to Joe Gans as the greatest fighter of his day." An Associated Press article quoted Nelson on a possible rematch with Gans: "Rather than allow a negro to dictate to me, I will give up the fighting game and retire forever."

Some writers redirected their prejudice ever so slightly, easily locating a target of bias within the sport, the ascendant heavyweight Jack Johnson. "Although Johnson talks bravely while out of the ring," R. A. Smyth of *The San Francisco Call* wrote, "he has invariably proved faint-hearted when put to the test in competition."

The subtext of Gans's story remained very much about race. Having freed himself from a white man's control, Gans encountered Tex Rickard, who deprived him of his rights during arrangements for the fight, and Nelson's manager Nolan, whose deviousness apparently continued after the fight. According to Dan Streible in *Fight Pictures: A History of Boxing and Early Cinema*, Gans said that Nolan, who distributed the fight film in some cities, manipulated the pictures to show Gans "in as bad a light as possible."

The film of the fight was well advertised. A typical notice read, "Original lifelike reproduction of the greatest battle ever fought in the history of the prize ring. Marvelous accomplishment of modern photography. Every move plain and distinct. Price for this engagement: entire lower floor 75 cents; first row in balcony 75 cents; remainder of balcony 50 cents." But Gans said that every move was not "plain and distinct" and that the missing parts would have shown how well he did. The New York *World*'s Barton Currie concurred: The footage did not reflect Gans's domination that he had witnessed at ringside. Rickard said that he had had the film shortened so that theater operators could find it more manageable. Whatever the case, *The World*'s editors sensationalized Currie's story with the headline FIGHT PICTURES WERE DOCTORED.

Gans had better luck in vaudeville. White show business operators would also make money at Gans's expense. But they paid well, and they took a chance with Gans. Soon after the Goldfield fight, Gans accepted an offer of $6,000 a month to appear on a midwestern circuit, a remarkable amount considering that two years later, baseball's Ty Cobb signed a contract for $4,000 for an entire season—and an $800 bonus only if he hit .300.

Theater operators hoped that Gans, despite his race, would be a drawing card. Boxers in vaudeville were almost exclusively white. "Gentleman Jim" Corbett recited monologues featuring Irish characters. In 1906 he played a repentant thief in *The Burglar and the Lady*, a play, and later a movie, written expressly for him. Jack London wrote a one-act play for Bob Fitzsimmons known by either of two titles, *Her Birth Mark* and *Her Brother's Clothes*. Jimmy Britt and Terry McGovern appeared regularly in vaudeville.

White audiences had had some exposure to black entertainers, notably jazz and opera singers, but not black athletes. Theater managers believed that Gans would attract customers because he was coming off an extraordinary fight, because he was a champion, because he was being talked about. All he had to do was to take a bow at the beginning or end of a show and box an exhibition of no more than three rounds against local competition. It was a pleasant way to make back part of his gambling losses.

His theatrical tour began in Duluth, Minnesota. Gans and

Martha Davis, after a trip to San Francisco to discuss his boxing future, caught the Overland Limited. At stops along the way, Gans waved to crowds that had heard he was passing through. In Minneapolis, he had to pay someone to be his "opponent"; when the master of ceremonies called for "all comers," no one left his seat. George A. Barton, a sportswriter and not a bad boxer, seized the moment and introduced himself to Gans:

> I asked him how much he paid and he said twenty-five dollars a day. I said, I'll be your sparring partner.
> He said do you box?
> I said I licked Terry McGovern.

To Barton, his beating McGovern was the best evidence that McGovern could not have knocked out Gans legitimately, and six years later he still was upset that Herford had talked Gans into the fix.

"Joe was a lovable fellow," Barton said. "He hired me. He just hit me enough to make it look good. But he never hurt me. I heard how he crossed a right hand over [his opponent's] left. I asked him to show me how he did it. Joe didn't want to do it. He was afraid he might hurt me but I finally convinced him. He hit me with that right over my left and my teeth gnashed together. But Joe held me up."

In St. Paul, the black community honored Gans with a dinner. He wore a handsome dark brown suit, and he never spoke of his victory over Nelson unless someone brought it up. When questioned about the fight, he told the audience: "It is not my desire to deprive Battling Nelson of any credit due him for our recent battle at Goldfield, but in fairness to all concerned I do not believe he is due very much, considering the adverse conditions under which he made me fight him."

In Milwaukee as well, black leaders held a banquet for him.

Saturday night festivities stretched into the early hours. The host's wife wore an elegant, flowing gown imported from Paris and a tiara of diamonds. A woman in a purple satin gown with large green satin bows who called herself "Queen of the Badlands" climbed up on a table and toasted the champion. When Gans said good night in the hall, women wept.

In Cleveland, he and a theater manager circumvented a law that prohibited boxers from giving demonstrations on stage—even John L. Sullivan had been barred from making an appearance there—by arranging a speaking part for Gans in a burlesque skit. After that, he gave a three-round exhibition with Kid Simms. Gans did not throw a hard punch, and Simms added to the show's hilarity by using pillows to defend himself.

The tour went smoothly until Cincinnati. That was where Madge Gans, then the current Mrs. Gans, had been raised. Having returned to visit relatives and perform in a chorus line in black vaudeville, she awaited her husband's arrival. By her account, her knock at his door was answered by Martha Davis, who slammed the door in her face.

Gans had so many stage appearances that it took him from early September to November 18 to reach Baltimore. There he found Madge Gans pressing for a divorce. The two had been separated for months, she said in court, and she would no longer abide his "frivolous conduct on the road."

27

On November 26, Gans received an offer to fight again. Mike Riley, a saloonkeeper in Tonopah, one town over from Goldfield, put up a purse of $20,000, with the winner receiving $12,000. Gans's opponent would be Herman Landfield, a Canadian-born Jewish boxer, who fought out of Chicago under the name Kid Herman. Boxers often appropriated the nickname Kid, which suggested strength and joie de vivre, and, with a nod to marketability, simplified a name or altered ethnicity: Eligio Sardiñas Montalvo was Kid Chocolate, Johnny Gutenko was Kid Williams, Okon Bassey Asuquo was Hogan Kid Bassey. Envisioning a holiday bonanza, Riley scheduled the Gans-Herman fight for New Year's Day 1907. It would be a fight to the finish for Gans's lightweight title. Gans considered the match easy money. Kid Herman was no Battling Nelson. Who was?

Rex Beach planned to be among the boxing writers at ringside. In 1906, he had made the bestseller lists with his novel *The Spoilers*, a story about government officials stealing gold mines from prospectors, an idea that came to him as he prospected for gold—unsuccessfully—near the Arctic Circle. As a change of pace from the book, he considered Gans an ideal subject for a magazine piece.

Beach pitched his idea to *Everybody's Magazine*, a monthly. He depicted boxing, violent and gruesome though it was, as a part of American life that needed to be examined. He told the editors that he would flesh out newspaper accounts by describing the scene and explaining the sport's appeal.

"I wish to go and do what has never been done before—report the psychology of this affair; tell of the strange crowd that will gather there, and diagnose that strange kink in the human brain which leads men from all sections of this land into the most inaccessible part of it, to see two naked boys fight with padded fists, though public opinion is so against the sport that it is tabooed in all but one or two corners of the United States."

Exaggerating wildly, he called the Tonopah fight "the biggest story in the world."

His proposal was accepted.

As it turned out, rough weather in Tonopah gave extra life to the story. Beach stepped off a train in late December "into the whirling snow that the desert wind whipped into our faces. I had always pictured a desert as the home of heat waves and burning sands, but this frozen gale flapped my fur coat about my legs, numbed my nose, and destroyed illusion utterly."

In an introduction to the article, the editors praised Beach's work as a "virile piece of writing" that explained why "unconstrainable souls" dared to venture into the wild for a prizefight and "what lusty passions are awakened in them?"—although Beach never addressed the matter of "lusty passions." And it was doubtful that many well-educated fight fans, whom he characterized as those "who brush their teeth and polish their nails," were stirred enough to "flock thither even from the edge of the Atlantic." Given the weather, it was almost impossible to get there.

Mostly, only hard-faced, gun-toting miners on sleds came. A few Nevada mine owners, recognizable in their fur coats, made it. Those who came in by train from California, according to one writer, appeared "benumbed." They "alighted on the scene of the battle looking like men who had been caught in a small avalanche and rescued, half frozen from a grave of snow."

It was Tonopah and Goldfield's worst weather ever, known as "the winter of death." Flu killed miners by the hundreds, and people chopped up telephone poles to keep warm.

Rickard made it from Goldfield and renewed acquaintances with Beach, with whom he had survived an Alaskan winter in not dissimilar elements; they had lived in tents and cabins, built fires, and welcomed spring by buying steamboat tickets away from there. Beach modeled a character in *The Spoilers*, the Bronco Kid, after Rickard.

"Philadelphia Jack" O'Brien, the light heavyweight champion and an interested spectator, escorted Beach to each of the fighters' training quarters. At Herman's final workout, Beach, like many boxing neophytes who watch a professional boxer train, was overly impressed. "I don't see how any man of his weight can whip him," he said to O'Brien.

O'Brien cautioned: "Don't judge till you've seen the other fellow."

O'Brien then led Beach through the driving snow to watch Gans.

"As we were admitted through locked doors, a roar as of a Gatling gun broke on our ears," Beach wrote.

Gans was punching the bag and I marveled at the sight, for he presented the most perfect type of the fighting-machine I have ever seen. He was thin-flanked and keen as a race-horse, his back and shoulders lean with the lean-ness that comes from perfect form and years of careful building. Every ounce was bulked where it does the most good, above the line of the trunks. His head was shaved, and his whole body, from heel to crown, was like a beauti-ful bronze statue, rippling with life, poised and balanced with that skill which no sculptor can command and which comes from endless contests and tireless training. His face was thin and hawk-like in profile, with less expression than a mummy's.

There was no waste about him, either in body or in movement; but at every blow the leather bag roared and the platform shivered . . .

He bore no scars on head or face or limb, his teeth were as white and even as if cast from porcelain . . . His skin was like brown satin.

Only . . . the bones at the back of his hands were bunched and crooked where he had shattered them and driven them together.

Both Gans and Herman surprised Beach with their civility. Generally, fighters and writers have always bonded before a fight, partly because talking to newcomers breaks the monotony of training for a boxer, while writers appreciate the access afforded by the sport's disorganization. Beach leaped to the conclusion that all fighters were "fine-appearing, quite on a par with literary people, and much healthier."

Gans was heavily favored, the odds 4 to 1. Herman's manager, Nate Lewis, confidently bet $1,200 that the Kid would last at least fifteen rounds. Later, Lewis met up with Gans on a Tonopah street and told him of his bet. "You better lay it off, Mr. Lewis," Gans said. "The fight will go eight rounds."

As they parted, Gans looked back and said: "Eight rounds, Mr. Lewis."

Gans had predicted that he would knock out Frank Erne in the first round of their rematch. And on the eve of his rematch with Max Schmeling, Joe Louis told Jimmy Cannon that he would win by a knockout in the first round. The trick for the writer is to judge the extent of the fighter's seriousness: Is he trying to intimidate the opponent or boost ticket sales, or does he mean exactly what he says?

Fight day in Tonopah brought an end to the snow but a temperature of zero. Most of the newspapermen warmed to their work by downing shots of whiskey in shacks heated by burning logs in large drum stoves. When they moved to ringside they felt a wind blowing through the gaps in the wood siding of the impressively named but hastily built Casino Athletic Club. Beach listened in on complaints from his new colleagues, the boxing writers. They were cold: They blew on their fingers and kicked their toes against the board siding that held up the ring. A man sitting next to Beach explained that there shouldn't have been any siding because it shut off the crawl space beneath the ring where newspapermen customarily scrambled to safety in case of trouble. "Suppose some guy back there got sore at the referee and made a gun-play, where could the newspapermen hide?" the veteran told the neophyte.

And then he said to Beach, "That's Mrs. Gans," pointing toward Martha Davis. In his story, Beach described "Mrs. Gans" as "a handsome, modestly gowned mulatto woman."

The ten-thousand-seat arena was sprinkled with 3,226 fans, a remarkable turnout given the weather. Most wore heavy coats and gloves. The fighters wore overcoats as they entered the ring. Gans weighed 132 pounds stripped, having made the weight easily. But a photograph taken of him before the fight, like the photograph of him that appeared in *The Salt Lake Herald* before the Nelson fight, revealed a drawn face, hollow cheeks. "I'm the best bet I ever was in my life," Gans insisted.

Herman was such an easy opponent that it was hard to tell if Gans had regressed. The only trouble he encountered was failing to hear the bell ending round two when he threw a late punch and the fans booed. But he shouted an apology to them, then went to Herman's corner and explained what had happened. The crowd cheered—with one exception, Rex Beach noted: "I heard a shrill voice at my back screaming: 'Go it, Herman! Kill the nigger.' A ten-year-old boy stood between his brother's knees, his tiny fists tight, his face flushed as with a fever. The sight sickened and shocked me more than anything I saw during the contest."

In the eighth round Gans landed several solid punches and then hit Herman cleanly with a right uppercut to the jaw. Herman fell forward onto his chest, almost flat. His trainer ran to the edge of the ring where the fighter lay facedown and shouted: "Don't give up, Kid. For God's sake, get together."

But Herman heard not a word. He was, indisputably, out.

Of Gans, Beach wrote: "Of all the yelling thousands, the calmest man was this gaunt, unsmiling negro who stood with his back to the ropes, the plaintive wrinkle puckering his brow suggesting that this was work for which he had no fondness."

And of Martha Davis: "His wife had sat unmoved throughout the contest, but as the white lad groped blindly for support before his collapse, she wrung her hands and cried: 'My God!'"

•

Gans went back on the vaudeville circuit. In the *Chicago Daily Tribune*, George Siler wrote that Gans had scarcely left it, likening Herman to a vaudeville opponent. "If some of the old-time fighters were alive and saw Gans or any of the other boxers who engage in vaudeville boxing stunts for big bunches of money, they would want to be born again."

Riley, the Tonopah promoter who had overlooked the possibility of snow and cold in his haste to replicate Goldfield's success and had to cover the $40,000 he'd spent on the building's construction and the $20,000 purse, spread the word that Gans had gambled away his entire $12,000. Gans denied the charge, but he acknowledged that he had left some of his earnings at Riley's saloon.

Gans made $1,000 a week boxing exhibitions at Miner's

Bowery Theatre in New York, and in several midwestern cities. In St. Paul, the agent for the touring Washington Society Girls Company, which was appearing on the same bill as Gans, made a room reservation for him at the Ryan Hotel. But when Gans went to register, the man behind the counter said he could not stay there.

"Why not?" Gans asked.

"I really can't accommodate you," the man said.

If he needed reminding, there it was: He may have won the fight at Goldfield, he may have changed the thinking of some he met, but he hadn't changed the world he traveled.

28

On October 29, 1907, Gans opened the Goldfield Hotel and Saloon in East Baltimore. It was a grand occasion. He invited friends from New York, Philadelphia, Washington, Norfolk, Atlantic City, and even as far as Chicago. Horse-drawn carriages were lined up for blocks, and white politicians and sports figures joined with blacks in the celebration. Champagne flowed, and whiskey sold for an exorbitant fifty cents a shot.

The three-story brick building included a twenty-two-room hotel, where Gans lived. He had a partner named Eddie Meyers, but the champion's presence attracted the crowds. "They were swinging doors then and, man, they used to swing all night," James Jackson, a bartender there, told a reporter. "On Friday and Saturday nights those doors were never still. People kept banging through and they all wanted to see the great Joe Gans."

The Goldfield was in the heart of an old, predominantly black neighborhood of identical narrow row houses with patchy brickwork, wide chimneys, and uneven roofs that sloped toward the sidewalk. It was called Old Town. The streets were cobblestoned and gaslit. On late summer afternoons, the smell of frying rockfish and shad wafted through the air, and when dinner was done, people sat out on their front stoops until long after the lamplighter had passed and twilight had faded.

Gans's Goldfield represented a place of equality. Almost a hundred thousand blacks lived in Baltimore, one-fifth of the population, but they were confined to one-tenth of the city's area. Most had migrated from the Deep South, but Baltimore was still a southern city and discrimination was widespread. Blacks had to own $300 worth of property and pay taxes on it or they could not vote, while whites faced no such requirement. Blacks found it difficult to buy a ticket to a vaudeville show—even to cordoned-off bad seating, which was all they were allowed—and often they were turned away from the box office when seats were available, forcing them to deal with a white scalper on the streets.

Gans and Meyers changed things to some extent. They both had been connected to a nearby saloon at 1108 East Lexington Street called the Middle Section Club—Meyers owned it and ran a poker game upstairs, and Gans played first base for the Middle Section Giants sandlot baseball team. The two went into business and had Coots Jones's dilapidated bar demolished to make way for their sparkling vision.

The Goldfield was painted gold, and the garish bricks served as a beacon at the corner of Lexington and Chestnut streets. The building stretched along Chestnut because Gans had to buy two adjoining row houses and have the walls knocked out after an architect failed to allow space for a big enough kitchen. The whole thing cost $35,000, five thousand more than Gans had anticipated, but everything was as stylish as he had planned.

Each first-floor window of the saloon, partially covered by green damask curtains, was inscribed with "Goldfield Hotel" in script. There was a polished mahogany bar, and behind it were heavy mirrors, pyramids of highly polished glasses, and cut glass decanters. The railing of the bar was brass, as were the footrest and six strategically placed spittoons. The room was bright, with the walls papered red and the ceiling painted white. Large photos of Gans hung on the walls: one of him weighing in before a fight in New York, another of him helping up Battling Nelson during the forty-two-rounder. There was a rathskeller beneath the saloon, and both stayed open twenty-four hours a day, six days a week. A late-night crowd would walk over from the nearby theater district. The patrons were both black and white—whites, too, wanted to meet a celebrity like Gans. The Goldfield was one of the first places in the country to welcome both races.

"People could come in any time and get a drink," the bartender James Jackson said. "They came a little slower after five a.m. but they kept coming."

The food was as good as that served in the dining rooms of Baltimore's finest white hotels. According to a prevailing joke, since Gans had abided by his foster mother's wishes and brought back the bacon from Goldfield, the menu featured bacon: bacon soup, bacon salad, bacon and eggs, plain bacon, bacon fritters, bacon pie, "bacon à la bacon." Actually, the oysters, soft-shelled crabs, Maryland fried chicken, Smithfield ham, spoon bread, and hot biscuits were Goldfield's Southern favorites. And the entertainment was even better.

Gans hired Eubie Blake to play the piano. Before the Goldfield opened, Blake had played ragtime in the parlors of local bordellos, notably Aggie Shelton's five-dollar house. He was young and wore short pants, and each time he worked he had to rent a pair of long pants for a quarter from a boy he knew at a pool hall. When his mother found out where he was playing, she literally wanted to kill him to free him from the devil and save his soul. "Now wait a minute," her husband said to her. The father and son talked, and the son pulled back the rug of his room and revealed all the dollar bills he had hidden—mostly tips from customers at Aggie Shelton's. He was making more money than his father, who worked as a stevedore on the docks. "Let me handle this," he told Eubie as they went downstairs.

"With the raising we've given him," Eubie's father reassured the mother, "none of that sin [will] rub off on a good Christian boy."

The Goldfield turned out to be Blake's first major step toward New York's cabarets and Broadway, where he teamed with Noble Sissle on songs for the likes of Sophie Tucker. Sometimes Eubie played all night at the Goldfield. He made up ragtime tunes—syncopated rhythms that later would influence jazz. He already was somewhat known for "The Charleston Rag"— "Memories of You" and "I'm Just Wild About Harry" were yet to come. He made up another rag: "The Goldfield Rag."

Gans and Blake had been boyhood friends, although Gans was nine years older. Eubie tagged along, even copying the way the young Gans dressed, with a turtleneck sweater. They had shot marbles together, and Eubie grew up idolizing Joe. As young men, however, they had a falling-out over a prostitute whom Blake thought he loved. Gans, likely attracted to the same woman, tried to break up the relationship, but he went about it badly. As Joe and Eubie played in a poker game on the second floor of a bar on Lexington Street, Gans insulted Blake several times by calling him "juvenile" and embarrassed him by mentioning the woman's name, suggesting his affair with her. Blake wanted to fight Gans on the spot, but others wisely held him off.

Blake took the job at the Goldfield not out of friendship but for the money, an unheard of $55 a week. Gans tried in vain to make amends. Knowing that Eubie liked stewed tomatoes, he made sure that stewed tomatoes were on the menu every day. "Don't sell all the stewed tomatoes," Gans would tell the workers. "Save some for old Eubie, but don't tell him I told you to do it."

When Eubie really fell in love, it was with a beautiful and smart and older—by two years—girl named Avis Lee, who lived with her grandmother in a fine black section near Druid Hill Park, on Baltimore's west side. When it came time for him to ask the grandmother's permission to marry Avis, Eubie emphasized his salary. But the older woman hesitated at his mention of the Goldfield. Thinking quickly, he won her over by noting proudly that his parents were "pillars" of the Israel Baptist Church. Eventually, she came to appreciate his status as the Goldfield's official house pianist.

The Goldfield always kept two pianists, the initial tandem being Blake and Boots Butler. But Butler died only a few weeks after the opening, and another local legend known as One Leg Willie succeeded him. "When people ask me who was the greatest popular pianist you ever heard, I always tell them it was One Leg Willie," Blake said.

His name was Willie Joseph, and he was missing a leg as the result of an ice skating accident. Eubie said that because of his race, Willie Joseph, who died young, was not allowed to record any of his music—Blake called it a "stain on this country, although I love this country."

As Blake told it, Willie learned at a conservatory in Boston and won its final competition, only to be told by a school official that he could not receive the award because he was "colored." His consolation was a love for ragtime, and at the Goldfield he would play Sousa's "Stars and Stripes Forever" in march time and then again, slowly, in ragtime. When people went to the Goldfield, they not only could meet the champ, they could listen to Eubie Blake and One Leg Willie. Something always seemed to be happening.

Bud Harris, a sparring partner of Gans, drew enough laughs with his jokes at the Goldfield to give up boxing and become a full-time comedian. A neighborhood character known as "Bayview" made a reputation playing craps there. Couples honeymooned at the Goldfield. George M. Cohan, touring with *The Yankee Prince*, and Eddie Foy, who was in *The Orchid*, stopped in. Congressmen rode the train over from Washington.

Jack Johnson was a regular. One week, he dropped in every night after appearing as a special attraction with a traveling burlesque show. He always drew a crowd. Once, when Johnson showed up to seek Gans's advice on a fight, people packed the saloon and others jostled for position on the sidewalk, where they stood several rows deep. After talking upstairs in Gans's parlor, the two fighters eventually came down to greet people. A hubbub ensued, a lot of pushing and shouting. Gans didn't mind the increased business. Johnson loved the attention, especially from the white people in the crowd. His next stop would be a local armory, where he would give a boxing exhibition, and after a time, he headed off in a carriage.

When he heard that George Dixon was down on his luck, Gans wired John L. Sullivan to ask if he knew the former featherweight champion's whereabouts so he could offer him a job as a bartender and greeter. Sullivan wrote a column for *The Boston Daily Globe* called "Jolts from 'John L.,'" and, on reflection, Gans should not have been surprised to be jolted by the man who once said, "Any fighter who'd get into the same ring with a nigger loses my respect." Sullivan accused Gans in print of seeking "free advertising" for himself and for his saloon.

Charles Luckeyeth Roberts frequented the Goldfield—the Luckey Roberts who would become the first Harlem pianist to be published and recorded, a bridge from ragtime to jazz who would live long enough to slow his "Ripples of the Nile" to a ballad called "Moonlight Cocktail," which Glenn Miller played and Bing Crosby sang.

At the Goldfield, Luckey Roberts exchanged ideas with Eubie Blake and took boxing lessons from Gans. In his last years, Roberts taught the sport at a New York YMCA, passing on what Gans had taught him.

•

Gans was the first black man in Baltimore to own an automobile. He bought a fifty-horsepower Matheson touring car at a New York showroom for $5,865 in cash. The model was a favorite of the wealthy in the first decade of the twentieth century. Gans's was bright red and adorned with the latest accessories, which he had requested: a canvas top, a French siren horn, a single-pane glass windshield, a clock, a speedometer, and a luggage carrier. He asked that a triangle be painted on the right-hand door with gold lettering: JOE GANS, GOLDFIELD HOTEL.

"I believe you should have shock absorbers on this machine," the salesman said.

Gans laughed and replied: "We are not accustomed to them in our business."

He had the luxury car shipped by rail to Baltimore and parked it near the Goldfield's front door, where crowds gathered to gawk at it. The Matheson became known as "the Red Devil." Gans told a friend: "I have had fitted to this car one of those French screechers, for I want everybody to get out of my way. It would not do for me to hit anybody, for that would be a sort of publicity which I would not want."

When he rode around the city in it, he tipped his cap to people. Once, though, he dashed up Charles Street doing more than the twenty-mile-an-hour speed limit, and when he passed Mount Royal Avenue with several passengers joyfully hanging on, he shouted a "merry ha ha" to a patrolman named Durfee. But Gans made the mistake of returning the same way, and Durfee waved him over.

In police court, Gans told Justice Grannan that he had three senators in the car who had to catch a train. "On your way back you did not have anyone," Grannan said. "Why did you go so fast? This fast automobiling is getting too dangerous, therefore, your fine is $25 and costs." Gans pulled $50 from a roll of bills and gave it to the magistrate.

Sometimes Gans hired chauffeurs, but they tended to be distracted by people on the streets who recognized the passenger. The drivers ran into things: a telegraph pole, a lamppost, a streetcar pylon.

He let friends borrow the car, too, but one crashed into the brick wall of Camden Station. Stanley Rushton, riding in the back seat, had wanted to buy a ticket to Toronto, to continue wooing, as chance would have it, a former girlfriend of Battling Nelson. People had just gotten off a train from Washington and were hurrying into the streets when the big Matheson jumped a curb. It knocked down a lamppost that struck Ida Fields of Westminster, Maryland, who was heading home. Rushton was thrown from the car and landed on the pavement. A crowd gathered, which usually happened when fires broke out, but this was unusual, a car crash. Fields, revived by a railroad doctor, suffered cuts and bruises and caught a later train. Rushton, the flying passenger, was just bruised. The driver was released on his own recognizance after explaining that his wheels had caught in the streetcar tracks on Camden Street and that he had swerved to avoid an oncoming trolley.

The accident cost Gans about $2,000 in repairs. "This machine has cost me a lot of time and trouble in the last few days," he said. "I guess it must be hoodooed."

But he kept it.

•

He would retire from prizefighting—that was Gans's mantra. He swore off the races at Pimlico. He insisted to anyone who asked that he had to tend to the Goldfield and that his fighting days were done. But it was clear from the day that Battling Nelson found his way to the Goldfield that Gans would fight him again.

One morning, about eight o'clock, Nelson walked in. Only a few people were left in the bar. James Jackson was busy polishing glasses and straightening things.

"I'd like to see Joe," Nelson said.

"Joe?" Jackson replied.

"Joe Gans. This is his place, ain't it?"

"Yeah, this is Mister Gans's place," Jackson said. "But you can't see him."

"Mister Gans is resting and he don't get up for strangers," a bystander said.

"I ain't no stranger to Joe. Just tell him 'Bat' is here. He'll see me."

They pretended not to know he was the famous "Battler." They were having fun at his expense. They liked the idea of a white man seeking an audience with a black man.

"Just tell your boss it's Battling Nelson. I'll wait here until he can see me."

Jackson eventually went upstairs to a back room to awaken Gans and tell him that he had a visitor: Battling Nelson.

A few minutes later, Gans appeared in pajamas, robe, and slippers. He greeted his adversary with an embrace and introduced him to the others. Then the two fighters sat and talked. Gans made known his demands: In any future bout, the division of the purse and any conditions that might be imposed would favor him. Nelson concurred, or at least he said he did. He wanted a rematch. The public wanted a rematch. There would be too much money in it for Gans to ignore.

29

Gans's foster mother had received a good deal of publicity for urging Joe to "bring back the bacon." Now Maria Gans—by virtue of his success, she was better known as Gans than Gant—made the newspapers again for another missive. He sent her a $6,000 check before the Herman fight and she had wired back: THANKS, KEEP STEPPING JOE.

The *Chicago Daily Tribune* picked up on the exchange. "Those who 'keep stepping' are the ones who succeed," the *Tribune* said. "It is only those who stop that fail." Her "homely but sage advice" applied to everyone because "competition is so intense and the rush for wealth so headlong and furious."

The *Denver Republican* turned her words into a poem:

Don't dally on the primrose way—
Keep stepping.
Court not a single wasted day;
Just think what Mrs. Gans would say,
And let this be your joyous lay—
Keep stepping!

Gans had bought her a new home on Baltimore's near west side, 1026 Argyle Avenue, not far from the Druid Hill Avenue house where she had lived with Madge and him. Many of Baltimore's streets were quiet, Argyle Avenue among them. She sat alone in the twilight's glow, confident that Joe would "bring back the bacon."

It was September 1907 and he was out in San Francisco about to fight Jimmy Britt. Negotiations for a second bout with Nelson had lagged, and Gans was drawn by the money he could make fighting someone as popular in San Francisco as Britt. The city, which was rebuilding after the earthquake and fire, was known as "the Cradle of Fistic Stars." Britt was referred to as "the Native Son," or "Sir James Edward." He was San Francisco's darling of the moment.

He strutted around in a Prince Albert coat and bowler hat and jauntily swung a cane. Like "Gentleman Jim" Corbett, Britt had learned to box at the Olympic Club. The son of a state senator, he had gained prominence in the ring with a prolonged amateur career, which young men of means could afford. Newspapers depicted him as the essence of manhood.

The white population thought nothing of his characterization of Gans as "133 pounds of black meat."

Gans himself was well known in San Francisco. He had won six bouts there, and fans believed he also had earned a victory in September 1904 when the referee ruled a draw in a nontitle bout with the welterweight champion, Barbados Joe Walcott—from him, half a century later, Jersey Joe Walcott, formerly Arnold Cream, took the name.

Gans and Britt had met before, in October 1904, but that fight was fixed in favor of Gans, as Herford had arranged a scheme with Willus Britt, Jimmy's brother and manager: Britt would strike a low blow and be disqualified, thus eliminating the embarrassment of being severely beaten in front of his hometown fans.

Gans told reporters in February 1906 that he had been involved in two fakes. His dive against McGovern didn't surprise anyone. The Britt fix of 1904 came as news—Britt's fans were skeptical of the story. Following the revelation, most newspapers published articles blaming Herford and exonerating Gans, although some papers branded Gans a lowlife. Several white fighters used the two fixes as an excuse for drawing the color line against him, saying they had nothing to gain by fighting him. Some fans reacted angrily toward him. Gans was surprised because he thought that confession would bring forgiveness.

The 1907 rematch with Britt came as a welcome diversion in San Francisco. Two days before the fight, the Cliff House, a seven-story Victorian château above Ocean Beach, burned down. Its destruction saddened San Franciscans. On Sunday afternoons, they had taken steam trains or ridden out in carriages and picnicked beneath it. The year before, when the earth had stopped shaking from the quake and the fires had burned out, people asked—as Churchill would inquire of St. Paul's Cathedral after the nightly London bombings later in the century—if the Cliff House was still standing.

Gans was favored, but Britt's local following thought otherwise and interest was high. Houdini, the actor Nat Goodwin, and Joaquin Miller, "the Poet of the Sierras," were among the more than eighteen thousand who gathered in Recreation Park, the city's baseball field. Four thousand were turned away. Some watched from a perch above the board fences: from rooftops, on telephone poles, on the flat surface of a big rock on the corner of Fourteenth and Dolores.

Martha Davis—"Mrs. Gans"—was there, and the newspapers would speculate that it was out of respect for her that there was none of the usual jeering of women who attended the fights. The first bell was delayed a half hour as Ben Selig, who had become Gans's advocate on the West Coast, demanded that the promoter show him the money he had guaranteed. Reluctantly, Jack Gleason went to his safe and pulled out bills and gold coins totaling $15,000.

Shortly after three o'clock, as the weather changed from cloudy and windy to sunny, Gans appeared in his corner, wearing a green flowered velveteen robe. A blue blanket was draped around him. He wore white satin trunks. Britt wore red trunks and grandly took his bows. A Los Angeles writer, Charles E. Van Loan, as had reporters in Goldfield before the Nelson fight and in Tonopah before the Herman fight, said that Gans looked old: "His cheekbones are prominent; there are hollows underneath them, and other hollows under his eyes."

Gans did look old. And that made what followed more painful for Britt's fans. Gans whipped "the Native Son" badly. The crowd even turned against Britt when he quit after the fifth round, claiming he had broken his left wrist on Gans's right elbow. Most suspected that Britt, bruised and cut, took the easy way out. Willus Britt rushed his brother away in a red car before four doctors who had examined the fighter could agree on the nature of his injury.

In *The Call*, R. A. Smyth tried to allay the injured pride of any who had taken Jimmy Britt's downfall personally: "It is not fair to measure Gans with the usual standards of the fighter. His style is so artistic that it rises above the commonplace and can be appreciated by anyone with an eye to grace in movement."

It was Gans's biggest payday. He received $16,156 in purse money, and about $20,000 including the bets he made on himself. Fighting a white man made a difference: He had been paid only $1,833.70 when he fought Walcott.

In Baltimore, someone rushed up to Maria Gans as she waited in the dusk on the front steps of her new home. Britt had quit. "It would only have been a question of a few more rounds before Joe would have finished him," she said.

Going inside, she added: "He can bring home the bacon and the ham and the whole hog this time."

30

Gans rested a few days in Oakland before taking the overnight "Owl" to Los Angeles. He had a guarantee of $9,000 to defend his lightweight title against George Memsic on September 27. Memsic posed little threat. Gans stayed out west for the money.

He would train in Arcadia, California, founded by "Lucky" Baldwin, the last of the "Bonanza Kings" who made their fortunes from California gold mining in the 1850s. Baldwin owned an eight-thousand-acre ranch beneath the San Gabriel Mountains. Gans could take his morning runs on the eucalyptus-lined dirt roads. The fruit trees smelled of California promise.

Elias Jackson "Lucky" Baldwin not only was lucky in his mining investments, he was lucky to be alive. He had been shot by one of his many paramours and shot again a decade later by the sister of a jilted lover.

His property included the two-story brick Oakwood Hotel, which featured hot and cold running water and a fireplace in each of its thirty-five rooms. The famous gravitated to the Oakwood in a preview of Hollywood glamour.

When Gans arrived, via the Pacific Electric Railway from downtown Los Angeles, Baldwin was busy having the original Santa Anita racetrack built. He loved racehorses, and his stable included the stallion Emperor of Norfolk, "the California Wonder," winner of the 1888 American Derby under the African American jockey Isaac Burns Murphy.

Gans settled into a bungalow near the hotel, where he enjoyed ideal training conditions. He had privacy when he wanted it, and in the evenings he could wander over to the Oakwood and listen to the music.

Memsic was also known as Jimmy Burns—Burns was considered a good fight name. By coincidence, his manager happened to be Tommy Burns, the heavyweight champion. When Gans and Tommy Burns met to make arrangements for the fight, Gans tried to goad him into defending his title against Jack Johnson. Johnson eventually would chase Burns, a Canadian, all the way to Australia and knock him out in December 1908 to win the heavyweight championship.

"It isn't necessary for me to fight a coon," Burns told Gans.

Gans replied, a bit more eloquently: "Well, you must think you are a good deal better than your fighter . . . for a man has no right to ask any one else to do what he will not do himself," he told Burns. ". . . To show you what I think of you, I will bet you any amount you may desire that Jack Johnson can beat you and I have never seen Johnson in action."

Burns made no bet.

Eddie Smith, sports editor of *The Oakland Tribune*, criticized Tommy Burns and other white boxers who dodged blacks: "The color line is a joke and was originated for the sole purpose of giving fighters who are afraid to meet the good colored men in their class a chance to back away from a tough fight by claiming the color line."

The *Los Angeles Herald* sent a reporter out to Arcadia to observe Gans in training, and the writer, in an article without a byline, said that Gans was cheered on in a training session by a black spectator identified as "one big boogie."

As for the fight, Gans had no trouble with Memsic. A sellout crowd of about five thousand watched in the barnlike Naud Junction Arena near downtown Los Angeles and seemed to appreciate the champion's boxing. He took no chance of being hit hard. Jim Jeffries, the retired heavyweight champion, worked as referee and rendered the obvious decision after twenty rounds.

"The only obnoxious feature of an evening of perfect sport," the *Los Angeles Herald*'s J. G. Griffen reported, was "a string of abuse" that Tommy Burns aimed at Gans from Memsic's corner.

The Washington Post observed: "The Baltimore negro is always received with a burst of cheers. Men overlook the color of his skin and see in him only the skillful boxer, the brilliant ring master, and the game fighter. Gans is to-day the best drawing card in the lists of pugilists. A fight with him is the highest honor to which any lightweight can attain. The people come to see Gans; they do not come to see a negro. The idea of a negro whipping a white man does not occur to the spectators. It is merely 'Gans beat so-and-so.'"

Still, when Gans made a guest appearance at Chutes amusement park in Los Angeles the weekend after he beat Memsic, he was billed as "the conqueror of the white race."

•

From September 1906 through September 1907 Gans earned— from fight purses, bets on himself, and vaudeville appearances— about $60,000, the equivalent, a little more than a century later, of almost a million and a half dollars. But he had regrets. He sounded wistful in a *Chicago Evening Post* article about Packey McFarland, a dark-haired up-and-comer. "My career has been an unusually long one for a fighter," he told *The Post*.

> In spots it has been bright, in others extremely dark and gloomy . . . All that I wish to say about the past is to call attention of the public to the fact that it has taught me some bitter lessons. It has taught me some things I would like to impart to not only Packey McFarland, but other

young men as well, young men who are starting out as he is, with excellent prospects . . . I would like to have my words carry to all young men . . . In my humble opinion, the greatest lesson learned from a harsh experience was this: Choose well your friends. Then stick to them.

What a pity it is, I am told, that I did not heed this earlier in my career. Those are indeed vain regrets. But I am trying my best to make amends at this time. I am decidedly careful in the selection of my companions now. Life in its most attractive form with a good, solid, honest background and foundation would have been mine now had I had the sense to recognize the so-called straight and narrow path ten years ago.

The *Indianapolis Freeman* wished Gans would stop fighting. It published a drawing of him as Alexander the Great, looking out across the seas at his vast domain, implying that he had no more worlds to conquer.

31

It should have come as no surprise that Joe Gans caught tuberculosis, though it has never been pinned down precisely when he
caught it. The disease, also called consumption at the time, was
widespread in the cities, and that is where he spent most of his
time. People realized he wasn't the same fighter when he fought
Nelson a second time on July 4, 1908, but they thought his age
was slowing him. Only later would it become public knowledge
that TB was the reason.

Most newspapermen—but only in retrospect—believed that
he carried the disease when he fought Nelson at Goldfield and
that by the time he left town, it had begun its deadly assault.
They wrote that the three weigh-ins before the fight and the
forty-two rounds in the blazing sun dehydrated him and caused
the tuberculosis germ in him to flare. They believed—a reasonable assumption—that, before Goldfield, he had become susceptible to the infection by repeatedly taking off weight to make the
lightweight limit of 133 pounds.

The rest of what they wrote was, for the most part, specula-
tive. Some believed he got infected as early as 1905. One writer
who knew him said that doctors told him before 1900 that it was
in his body. He could have gotten it in a gym or by just being out
in the crowds of Baltimore or New York. It's conceivable that he
contracted it as early as 1896 from his second wife, Mary Beulah, who died of TB that year.

It was possible to live for years with tuberculosis. The poet Paul Laurence Dunbar died of TB in 1906 at the age of thirty-three, six years after he had been diagnosed.

A man named Jimmy Dougherty, who trained boxers and refereed fights, believed that tuberculosis had begun to take a toll on Gans in late 1905 before he set out for the West Coast without Al Herford. Before he went, Gans made a side trip to Leiperville, Pennsylvania, near Chester. He went there to borrow money from Dougherty, whom Damon Runyon nicknamed "the Baron of Leiperville."

An affable host, Dougherty used to invite over Bob Fitzsimmons's wealthy friend Anthony Joseph Drexel Biddle, Philadelphia A's catcher Mickey Cochrane, Runyon, and H. L. Mencken. Over the years, Gans had trained in Dougherty's ring in Leiperville, and Dougherty was happy to have him.

According to Dougherty, Gans hoped to get enough cash to get to Chicago, where someone would give him the balance for the railroad fare to the coast. Since there was more boxing action there, Gans reasoned, maybe he could pick up some fights and make some money. During his visit with Dougherty, Gans admitted he wasn't feeling well.

Dougherty consented to a loan, but he persuaded Gans to go with him to his doctor to be examined. Afterward, the doctor took Dougherty aside.

"Didn't you tell me this man was some sort of an athlete?" he asked.

"That's right. He's a boxer, the lightweight champion of the world."

"Impossible," the doctor said. "Why, he is not only in advanced stages of tuberculosis, but he has other serious ailments. He should be in bed."

For Gans to fight forty-two rounds under the desert sun in the advanced stages of tuberculosis would seem unlikely, and a doctor's examination on the eve of the fight found him perfectly fit; included in his detailed statement was the phrase "lungs normal in every respect." But Dougherty took his story to the grave.

Two things can be said for certain:

Gans had tuberculosis in some form when he fought Nelson the first time. Sally Zanjani, in writing about Goldfield, said that Gans "suffered from undiagnosed tuberculosis" going into the forty-two-rounder. The sports historian Steven A. Riess has written: "Gans fought only twice in 1905, having contracted tuberculosis." Jim Tully wrote that Gans at Goldfield was "even then in the grip of tuberculosis" and that he "went into the ring a fading black shadow of a man."

The second truth: There is no doubt that his tuberculosis had become active before his second fight with Nelson.

Some people had to know. Martha Davis, for one; his associates, Kid North, perhaps. Al Herford must have known when he let him go; Bob Edgren of New York's *The World* had "little doubt" Herford knew.

Gans spent the early part of 1908 fighting lesser opponents, as if nothing was wrong. Among the bouts: He knocked out a man named Blackburn—or Blackburn simply lay down for the count—as part of a fund-raiser in Baltimore for Herman Miller, a boxer who, ironically, was dying of TB; Gans knocked out Rudy Unholz in San Francisco, but of greater interest is a photograph taken beforehand in which Gans seems anything but sickly—he looks perfectly healthy, handsome.

Over the years it has been written that when Gans went to the ring for his rematch with Nelson he was a dying man. But at fight time, few knew Gans was sick. He was a 10-to-3 favorite.

32

In June 1908, Joe Gans's rematch with Battling Nelson finally was on. Ben Selig, Gans's representative, and Willus Britt, whom Nelson had hired to replace Billy Nolan as his manager, met in an Ellis Street saloon in San Francisco and negotiated a contract for a forty-five-round bout on Saturday afternoon, July 4, at Coffroth's arena.

James W. Coffroth had built the wooden Mission Street Arena a year earlier just fifty feet across the San Mateo County line, in Colma, to free himself from interference from San Francisco city officials. He came to be known as "Sunny Jim" because his bouts, held in daytime, usually enjoyed favorable weather.

It's not known how Martha Davis felt about Gans's decision to keep fighting. As the most influential person in his life, she may have advised him to retire, and he ignored her. It's possible, but not likely, that she didn't mind if he continued.

Gans set up camp across the bay at Billy Shannon's Villa in San Rafael. Shannon's Villa enjoyed mythic status in prizefight circles but was less romantic than it sounded. It was a plain wooden building with training quarters for boxers and a saloon. Patrons could watch the sparring, have a drink, and talk about the fighters, or talk directly with them. Shannon had relocated to the country from San Francisco's South of Market district after the earthquake and fire, and the likes of Jim Corbett and Jim Jeffries, Nelson and Jimmy Britt, Kid Lavigne and Frank Erne trained at one or the other of Shannon's places.

Gans would meet Nelson fifty-one days after the Unholz fight, plenty of time to train. The problem was Nelson. Gans knew it was almost impossible to knock him out. He called Nelson "the toughest of them all."

Smyth, the writer for *The Call* who had covered the Goldfield fight, had heard Gans's appraisal of Nelson but asked him anyway. Gans responded: "If you take a group of artists you will find one has a touch of genius. The same is true of writers. One has a touch of genius and his work will stand out above that of other men. Nelson seems to have this peculiar quality, but in him it takes the form of being able to resist blows that other men could not stand."

As he had before his fight with Unholz, Gans looked fit in a photo, posing with a group on the steps of Shannon's home. In the evenings, Kid North would play the piano in the Villa and shout ragtime. Gans and other boxers and sparring partners would gather around the piano and request tunes such as "Tricks Ain't Walkin' No More."

But as happy as Gans seemed, Smyth suspected all was not right. The reporter had seen enough of him training in Goldfield to know that there was a change. Now Gans rarely put on gloves. He spent most of his time running the dirt roads around San Rafael, claiming that he did not have to improve his boxing skills. He said—and here was an indication that he lacked strength—the most important thing he could do was to build his stamina. He sparred only three times before the fight.

Smyth thought back to Gans's fight with Unholz. While virtually everyone believed it had been an effortless victory, Smyth wrote at the time that Gans "showed some sign of distress."

Smyth decided after seeing Gans at San Rafael that age was hampering him. He needed to train harder for Nelson, Smyth wrote, taking exception to Gans's attempt "to condition himself with the least possible strain."

"He cannot afford to baby himself trusting his ability to stop Nelson within a reasonable number of rounds. The Dane has been a surprise to many opponents in his time, Gans among them, and the latter will have to be ready for a hard fight."

•

On the morning of the fight, people crowded onto the Mission Street trolleys and rode to the end of the line at the city's edge. The short walk from there to the arena resembled a bustling open-air market. Beggars knelt at the side of the dusty road, men and boys sold sandwiches and scalped tickets, other men operated gambling games, using tomato cans as dice cups. Mounted police kept the crowd moving.

A big auto pulled up to one of the arena's entrances. It was Gans, arriving with Martha Davis. He wore an overcoat and cap and looked perfectly calm. She wore a dark dress and a large black hat with a veil. The way was parted for them and they went inside. Gans had been defeated merely three times spanning the previous seven and a half years. But that morning, Smyth's story included a fateful line: "It may be that the wonderful vitality which has carried him through so many fights has been sapped."

Think of great champions growing old: Joe Louis and Archie Moore—Joe's bald spot, Archie's flab—and Sugar Ray Robinson when he was forty-four years old, his trunks slipping as he struggled to beat someone who called himself Young Joe Walcott. Or Muhammad Ali, covering both sides of his head with his arms as he was beaten into retirement.

Had it been possible to have persuaded any of them not to fight again, one would have. But old boxers think of past glories and in their own way inform Tennyson's words: "'Tis not too late to seek a newer world." They might land a lucky punch.

33

"The fight crowd is the most unreasoning, unjust, vicious, and vindictive of the audiences of sport," W. C. Heinz once wrote.

The crowd at the second Gans-Nelson fight, or at least a portion of the nine thousand, fit the description.

People swarmed into the ring and, storming past Gans, lifted Nelson onto their shoulders. Their euphoria, at least in some cases, had to come from a sense of relief: A white man had beaten a black in a title fight. Nelson raised his right arm and held it up, and laughed. He was lightweight champion of the world.

On the other side of the ring, a woman climbed between the ropes and rushed to her fighter's side. He sat slack on his stool. She threw her arms around his neck and held him close. "Never mind, dear, never mind, you are all right. You fought like a man. Remember, I am always with you."

Joe Gans looked up at Martha Davis but said nothing. His eyes were glassy and, frighteningly to those around him, he shook uncontrollably, as if a great chill had taken hold of him. It was a sign of tuberculosis.

His seconds bundled him and helped him down the steps of the ring. He continued to shake. They laid him on a couch in a dressing room. Martha Davis held tight to his hand and helped wipe the blood from his face.

The writers assembled in the room. They stood there awkwardly. They could feel the heartbreak. In the dressing room of the loser, sometimes it feels as if time has stopped.

"Napoleon met his Waterloo and now Joe's time has come," Martha Davis eventually told the massed media. "Joe was the best of them all for so many years that it is hard for him to lose now. But I guess he will have to make the best of it. Nelson was too strong and too young for him."

Her words made sense. She kept her explanation to the matter of age. Joe was thirty-three. Nelson had turned twenty-six a month earlier. Joe was better off at home, thinking back to all the boxing he had done and feeling good about it.

She didn't say anything about tuberculosis. She didn't mention that he might have been fighting with only one working lung, maybe even with one lung collapsed and the other badly damaged.

Reporters didn't know what the trouble was, but some noticed a difference in Gans early in the fight. During the first round, one writer remarked: "Gans is feeling the effects of age, and he cannot come back with his old quickness. He is a beaten man unless he improves." Another expressed surprise that Gans "stood straight up and smashed Nelson with terrific blows on the chin" because he looked "gaunt . . . like a dead man even in the early rounds."

Gans tried for the first five rounds to knock out Nelson, knowing he couldn't last forty-five rounds. He outboxed Nelson and bloodied his face, the blood splattering on Nelson's chest. But unlike the first five rounds at Goldfield, this time Nelson landed several hard blows. As early as the minute between the third and fourth rounds, Gans told his corner men that he was tiring. And by the sixth round, Nelson took charge. He bore in relentlessly, punched relentlessly, punished relentlessly. In the seventh round, he unloaded often to the head; uncharacteristically, Gans offered no defense. Nor did he ever retaliate until a short-lived rally during the tenth round, which he won, raising his fans' hopes.

In the eleventh round, he seemed listless. And in the twelfth, Nelson knocked Gans to the floor three times. The most telling punches landed in his midsection and bent him over. Nelson pounded him . . . down, down, down.

One reporter wrote that Gans's skin turned a dull gray and that he shivered as though from a fever.

In the thirteenth, Nelson sent him sprawling again.

In the sixteenth, too. In the sixteenth, Gans trembled.

In the seventeenth, Nelson whaled away, most often to the stomach. He hit Gans as if he were trying to beat him to death. Gans fell once, twice, three times—now he had been knocked down eight times during the fight. This is what Joyce Carol Oates must have meant when she wrote that boxing was beyond the "perimeters of civilization."

Gans tried to regain his feet. He could have made it, it seemed. But he did not hurry. He knew what he was doing, making the effort slowly. Jack Welch, the referee, counted to ten.

"Oh, my Joe," Martha Davis cried. "Oh, my Joe."

Nelson was "the happiest man in America"—so he recalled in the "Introductory" to his autobiography.

In Baltimore, a crowd overflowed the Goldfield into the street. Inside, a man shouted developments from the AP's blow-by-blow account. Another man stood in the doorway with a megaphone and relayed the news. There came the final words: Joe Gans was knocked out.

How could Nelson have beaten Joe? How could anyone beat him? Was it age?

His followers drifted away. There was despair in the dusk.

If the forty-two-rounder at Goldfield had taken something from Nelson—and it surely did, for he would never be the same fighter afterward—it had stolen more from Gans. What the fight and TB together took is incalculable. To Smyth, he looked like "an old, old man."

Meaning to compliment Gans, Rube Goldberg wrote in *The San Francisco Call*—*the* Rube Goldberg, who would be known for his cartoons of complex devices that performed simple tasks: "He displayed a quality of gameness that would be a credit to any white man in the fighting business today."

The evening of the fight, Gans took the ferry back to San Rafael. When he got off, he was still shaking.

34

There's no good reason why Gans remained in San Francisco after he'd lost the way he did to Battling Nelson.

Had he known the fates of some of his black contemporaries, which had yet to play out, he might have understood better the ravages of prizefighting. But Sam Langford was still decades away from tapping his white cane down the streets of Cambridge, Massachusetts. And Joe Walcott, to whom New York mayor Jimmy Walker gave a custodial job at Madison Square Garden, a bad enough ending in itself, would disappear in 1935, apparently to be killed by a car while walking on a road in Ohio.

Two nights after he had been beaten badly, Gans agreed to a third bout with Nelson. Ben Selig and Willus Britt met and planned it. Tex Rickard offered a $30,000 purse to promote it and proposed a fight to the finish in Ely, Nevada, on Labor Day, September 7. They all had witnessed Gans's condition after Nelson had tortured him, but it didn't matter to them. The fight had made money. Nelson received $10,093.02, Gans $6,728.68, and Coffroth about $5,000. A third fight could make money, too, and Gans wanted it, as if he didn't consider his health important. In fact, this time he wanted $10,000, and Rickard got it for him. He persuaded Nelson to give Gans $5,000 of the $25,000 he commanded in exchange for Gans's giving up his share of the profits in the fight films. Rickard planned to divide those with Nelson.

Selig recommended that Gans vacation for several weeks in the clean air of the California mountains—clean mountain air was the prescription for those infected with tuberculosis. It was an odd time for Martha Davis to leave him, but she traveled to Portland, Oregon, supposedly to visit friends for a month. Again, she might have pleaded with him to stop. Maybe she could bear no more. Maybe she felt there would be nothing to miss in training. Why she went away is a mystery.

Gans had never been on vacation. He went up into the mountains, to Middletown, ninety-one miles north of San Francisco, to an elevation of about eleven hundred feet. He went on two deer hunting outings, rode horses, slept outdoors on a veranda, took sulfur baths, and developed an appetite that had been missing. He built himself up to about 144 pounds, telling Selig, when he visited, that he felt better than he had in years. Selig urged him to stay there until only days before the fight. Billy Nolan, Nelson's former manager who had caused Gans so much trouble at Goldfield, owned a ranch in the mountains and detected "a wonderful change" in Gans's condition. Nolan marveled that Gans was "all life and animation."

Nelson, meanwhile, soaked in his celebrity. As he walked along the San Francisco waterfront, small boys ran after him and shouted, "There is the new champion!" He put that in his autobiography. Also that he "could not help getting wider around the chest."

He was hailed as the new champion everywhere he went: from San Francisco to Livermore, California, where he had bought some land, to Ely, Nevada, to Chicago, to his home in Hegewisch, to New Mexico. Bands played "Hail to the Chief." In Obar, New Mexico, east of Albuquerque, he was awakened in his Pullman berth at three o'clock in the morning by gunfire celebrating his arrival. In Tucumcari, New Mexico, he received a .45 pearl-handled revolver and was made a deputy sheriff. Back in

San Francisco, he was honored with a dinner for four hundred people at the Fairmont Hotel.

Nelson vowed to show Gans no mercy.

This time, Nelson would be the favorite—the opening odds were 10 to 8. This time, the newspapers referred to Gans as "the old boy," "the old black boy," "the once great 'Old Master.'"

There was no stopping the fight from being held, even when Rickard bowed out as promoter. In late July, he claimed he could not arrange for special low railroad fares for fight fans traveling from Salt Lake City to Ely. But that would have meant Rickard had suddenly lost his ability to charm. Not likely. It is possible that Rickard had been conscience-stricken about promoting a fight involving a man as sick as Gans. Not likely either. "Gameness," which was all that people could expect from Gans, was not enough to guarantee a successful promotion. Rickard sensed that people would not go out of their way to travel to Nevada for a third Gans-Nelson fight. It was about money, and Rickard realized he would make little of it.

Coffroth stepped in. He switched the fight's location from Ely to his Mission Street Arena. With a larger population to draw from, he would be taking less of a risk. He scheduled the fight for forty-five rounds, with the winner and loser receiving percentages of the gate. Having already scheduled a featherweight championship bout at his arena on Labor Day, he planned Gans-Nelson for September 9—Admission Day, a statewide holiday marking California's entrance into the Union in 1850.

In mid-August, the fighters settled into training in Bay Area gyms. Gans came down from the mountain and went to Croll's in Alameda, next to Oakland, which he said would be cooler than San Rafael. Nelson worked at Millett's in Colma. Every chance he got, he beat up his sparring partners.

People still wanted to see Gans, and on a Sunday afternoon, four thousand people flocked to Croll's for a sparring session.

Men and boys climbed trees to watch the workout. And he showed them why he had been champion for so long, as ill as he was. And he was ill.

The *Chicago Daily Tribune* reported that he had developed "a tendency to tuberculosis," although the paper hardly trumpeted the news: The *Tribune* gave it one paragraph. On August 21, under the headline HAS JOE GANS TUBERCULOSIS? the newspaper said that before he left Baltimore for the West Coast—before his second fight with Nelson, on July 4—Gans "was in worse shape than many of his acquaintances imagined and that he would come home to fight the toughest battle of his life—a struggle with [the] disease." The *Tribune* said he was "drying up" and losing weight, and that a doctor had ordered him to sleep outdoors.

In a letter to Al Herford back in Baltimore, Gans asked that he bet him "for old times' sake."

On the day of the fight, Jay Davidson of the *Los Angeles Herald* wrote that Gans physically did not look nearly as good as his aides and the promoter had advertised, that he was "not the Gans of two and three years ago by a whole lot," that he was "all in," that Nelson would punish him, that Nelson could hurt him.

It was all true. Gans won the first round, although immediately afterward Willus Britt shouted to him from Nelson's corner: "If you can't hit any harder you might as well quit." But Gans won the fifth and seventh rounds, and he even managed to win the sixteenth. It was stunning that he could win a round that late, or even that the fight had lasted that long.

Nelson smiled. He smiled often. He would jog back to his corner after a round. After the eleventh, Gans had trouble finding his corner. His seconds pleaded with him to stop. They wanted to throw in the sponge, but he continued to tell them he would fight as long as he had the strength to stand up. His persistence and his pride prolonged the fight.

And that prolonged the punishment.

In the fourteenth round, Nelson shoved Gans between the ropes and out onto press row. The newspapermen pushed him back. During the fifteenth, Gans looked too exhausted to continue. That had to be the end, spectators thought. But no, the fifteenth and sixteenth rounds came and went, and so did the seventeenth and the eighteenth and the nineteenth.

At the bell ending the twentieth round, Gans knew he had covered the bets of those who had thought the fight would last twenty rounds or more. His right eye was closed. His left eye was almost closed. His face was puffed. His lips and nose were cut. But Nelson hadn't knocked him down. Not yet.

In the twenty-first round, however, Nelson landed thunderous rights and lefts to the stomach. Gans dropped to his knees. He tried to get up but fell back on his knees. He tried again as Eddie Smith, the Oakland newspaperman and referee, counted. Gans wobbled as he rose. He used all the strength he had to stand. And he managed to. But he was late. He had been counted out.

The New York *World*'s account included this: "When in the twenty-first round of his third fight with Battling Nelson, old Joe Gans yesterday sank to the prize ring floor from sheer weakness, he proved that his black skin hid a bulldog courage that some white men have hitherto denied him."

Nelson declared that he would never fight "a colored man" again—none was worthy of him, he said.

And in his autobiography, he included a cartoon labeled "Battling Nelson's Colored Morgue." Cad Brand of the *Milwaukee Sentinel* drew it, five black fighters in caricature, stretched flat and looking up at their conqueror with silly smiles. The rightmost figure is "Joe Gans," and above his head is Nelson's claim of *three* victories over him.

The drawing is captioned "Bat Nelson, 'Coon Hunter.'"

35

On July 17, 1908, Circuit Court No. 2 in Baltimore granted Madge Gans an absolute divorce from the former champion. They had been estranged for years, having separated in November 1904, when he'd roamed the country and she, reluctantly, moved from Baltimore to Chicago, where she would run a boardinghouse on Wabash Avenue.

On Saturday, October 3, 1908, Gans married Martha Davis at his Goldfield Hotel, in Baltimore. A reception followed. Al Herford served as master of ceremonies. Gans hoped that his name linked again with Herford would not hurt his chances of boxing—Herford was persona non grata in New York, and New York was where Gans was thinking of looking for another opponent. As beaten as he'd been, as ill as he was, he believed he still could go a few rounds if the money was right.

36

In East Baltimore, friends of Gans found it hard to imagine him as an innkeeper when boxing had been his life. But it was harder for them to think about the punishment that Nelson had given him. It made sense to them when he said he planned to tend to his hotel and saloon and was retiring from boxing. "I've positively fought my last battle," he said.

He gave $100 toward a monument to be built in George Dixon's honor. He gave $100 for survivors of an earthquake in southern Italy, knowing not a single Italian but understanding earthquakes' devastation. He gave $100 for a monument to the late deputy fire chief of New York, who in 1904 had ordered seven fire trucks loaded onto flatcars in Jersey City in case they were needed in Baltimore when much of the city burned down; Gans took particular pride in that donation because it matched that of J. Pierpont Morgan.

The white press depicted him as "a hero to his people." One article said that he had overcome "bitter prejudice" by his "quiet, reserved deportment and careful regard for the feelings of others" and that his manners did more to help "the negroes get a square deal from the American public" than any reformer.

But Gans was restless. He wanted to fight again. In October 1908, he made known his desire. But he placed restrictions on a prospective bout. He would fight only six or ten rounds. He would fight only in the East, claiming he could not leave his busi-

ness for long, when actually he could not withstand a lengthy trip
without tiring.

Sunny Jim Coffroth believed he could successfully promote
Gans once more in San Francisco, and he proposed a twenty-five
rounder against Packey McFarland on New Year's Day 1909.
Gans knew better. He wired regrets.

That January, a Philadelphia promoter offered him $2,500 to
fight six rounds with Young Erne, an undistinguished lightweight
who took his name from the champion Gans had knocked out in
1902. He accepted. But ten days later, he had to cancel. He was
sick. *The New York Sun* reported the illness as "neuralgia of the
heart." Gans was confined to his suite at the Goldfield for four or
five days, and a doctor said he needed another two weeks before
he could even discuss the possibility of boxing.

On February 14, Theodore Roosevelt invited Battling Nelson
to the White House as one of his last guests before William
Howard Taft was sworn in as president. Gans's reign coincided
with Roosevelt's years as president, but Roosevelt extended no
such invitation to the man who would have been more conver-
sant than Nelson in the science of the sport. Roosevelt called
Nelson "a stanch friend."

That month, Gans returned to New York, and this time he
got himself a ten-rounder against an Englishman named Jabez
White. The fight was scheduled for March 12 at the National
Athletic Club on East Twenty-fourth Street in Manhattan, and it
would be advertised as an exhibition because prizefighting in
New York was illegal at the time. Gans would be paid $2,500,
having persuaded the club's manager to raise his first offer of
$2,000. One boxing writer dubbed White "a back number" who
"could not hit hard enough to make a dent in a piece of putty."

Three days before the fight, Gans arrived in New York at
midday. He ran in Central Park and then went downtown by
horse and carriage to work out at the National A.C. Traveling

Fifth Avenue, he admired the size of the buildings—some more than twenty stories—and felt the energy of the city. Another million people had moved in since 1900, when he had last spent significant time there.

The New York Times opposed the bout because it would be between a black man and a white man. *The Times* would declare before the Jack Johnson–Jim Jeffries fight that it was not a good thing for the two races to meet in any kind of competition and advised readers to "hope that the white man may not lose." The newspaper said it would wait "in open anxiety that he has licked the—well, since it must be in print, let us say the negro, even though it is not the first word that comes to the tongue's tip."

The New York police commissioner, Theodore Bingham, said he would try to stop the Gans-White fight from taking place. But Tim Sullivan and his Tammany cronies controlled the club, and on fight day itself, Bingham was more interested in crushing the Italian underworld than stopping a fight because, on that very day, his best Italian informer, Giuseppe Petrosino, was shot and killed by Mafia assassins in Palermo, Italy.

The Times reported that a "big crowd" went to see Gans-White. Jim Jeffries, Sam Langford, Stanley Ketchel, Abe Attell, and Nelson were there, their presence an unspoken tribute to Gans. It was a dreadful contest, and it dragged on for all ten rounds.

"Gans was shot through and through with tuberculosis," Charley Rose, the matchmaker for the undercard, said. "But the National doctor passed him."

Gans had little strength. He and White were slow, their punches weak. Both were breathing hard by the middle rounds. The crowd hissed. Gans managed to knock White down twice in the sixth round, once in the seventh when he was saved by the bell, and once in the eighth. When both fighters finished on their feet, the referee ruled no decision, which was required by the

New York law of the moment. The newspapermen awarded their own decision, and Gans got it.

But almost everyone was puzzled by Gans's inability to knock out White. Uncharacteristically, Gans had swung and missed and hadn't followed up his opportunities. Some thought he intentionally let White finish on his feet. Others, among them William P. McLoughlin of the *St. Louis Post-Dispatch*, believed that his skills had eroded terribly. McLoughlin described Gans as "merely a shell of his old self," saying that he was in such bad shape "any kind of a punch would have put him down for the full count and then some."

Back in Baltimore, Gans said he hadn't trained. The reason he gave to friends and a few reporters at the Goldfield was flimsy. He said the city had taken away his saloon's liquor license and that he had spent most of his time worrying about it and trying to get reinstated. He also admitted to having a nagging cold. He seemed susceptible to colds.

The next day, Gans begged off visiting a boxer training in Berwyn, Maryland, near Washington, and stayed in bed at the Goldfield.

Before the month was out, Charlie White, the referee, was quoted by the Associated Press as saying that Gans had contracted tuberculosis and that he might never fight again. Gans's wife denied White's claim. Gans also denied it. And he made light of it.

That summer, while visiting the office of *The Chicago Defender*, he told staff writers that he had spent hundreds of dollars on physical exams that would have been better spent at the racetrack. "They told me over in Baltimore that I had consumption," he said, feeling good that day, "but I find now that it was all a joke."

37

George Bellows liked to paint what was topical, and mixed-race prizefights were certainly that in 1909. Newspaper articles by the score were devoted to the subject, most of them in favor of keeping the races separate. Bellows's opportunities to see a black man and a white man fight were few and growing fewer because the white public was calling for an end to interracial bouts as soon as a white man could beat Jack Johnson. Bellows relished using his talent to contradict popular opinion.

He realized white America's hatred of Johnson. As a sports fan, he would have known about Gans's career, and it would have been easy for him to head downtown from his midtown Manhattan studio to see Gans fight Jabez White. Bellows's mentor, Robert Henri, had suggested that he get out on the streets of New York and paint all aspects of life, especially the gritty side, and Bellows often said that he painted only what he saw. That included construction workers, poor boys swimming in the East River, prostitutes. He believed they told the story of America as definitively as the rich.

He liked going to the fights. Normally, he had only to cross the street from his top-floor studio in the Lincoln Arcade Building, at the corner of Broadway and Sixty-fifth Street, to see prizefighters trading punches. "A fight, particularly under the night light, is of all sports the most classically picturesque," he decided after watching two men battle in the glow of Sailor Tom Sharkey's saloon.

Seven months after Gans-White, Bellows unveiled one of his masterpieces, *Both Members of This Club*. The title of the work stems from the practice of granting "membership" in a "club" to the fighters for the duration of their contest—as Ellison wrote about and Herford practiced in Baltimore. *Both Members of This Club* depicts a black boxer and a white boxer in a prizefight. Bellows found it ironic that a black fighter could gain instant equality not only with the white fighter but with the whites in the audience, whose self-importance he punctured by drawing them in guffawing caricature. He has the bloodied white fighter about to be toppled, suggesting, perhaps, that the black fighter is worthiest of all.

The painting hangs in the permanent collection of the National Gallery of Art. "The black contestant is Joe Gans, lightweight champion for eight years," the gallery's online description states. But gallery officials, when asked about the identity of the black figure in the painting, said it "could be" or "might be" Gans. Art historians say the black figure's identity is unknowable. Marianne Doezema suggests in her book *George Bellows and Urban America* that the painting "may represent a fight witnessed at an athletic club in another part of the city, which the artist then set in the environment he knew well from repeated visits to Sharkey's . . . The point is that Bellows self-consciously introduced race into his fourth boxing picture, thus intensifying the already volatile nature of the subject."

Of course there's doubt as to whether he drew the black figure—muscular but lithe, like a lightweight—after seeing Gans's fight, or simply on his knowledge of Gans; Bellows could even have gone to a theater and seen a film of Gans fighting. Bellows left few clues about the painting, and those who might have known its origin, or even where he was on the evening of March 12, 1909, are long since dead.

There is a clue, however, that Bellows was thinking of Gans when he painted *Both Members of This Club*. The black figure is a counterpuncher; many black fighters were trained to be counterpunchers so as not to throw the first punch at a white opponent. But Gans perfected the technique, which is noted in the National Gallery's description: "Gans's famous 'right punch after blocking a lead' may have led Bellows to record that maneuver for its own sake."

38

From summer 1909 to spring 1910, Gans often looked as if he could still be champion of the world. He spent much of his time in the Goldfield's saloon, talking to customers. He drove his "Red Devil" Matheson around town. But on those days when he did not look well, when he lacked energy and felt weak, he tucked away in his suite at the Goldfield. No one saw him.

Most of the newspaper stories about him concerned his health. Like the item in *The Washington Times*: "Reports come from Baltimore that Joe Gans is plainly suffering from consumption, and that he has not many months to live." Or a contradictory two-paragraph blurb in the *Richmond Times-Dispatch* under the headline JOE GANS IS GOOD FOR MANY YEARS.

He had been down in the Old Dominion, giving boxing exhibitions at a theater in Petersburg, creating the notion that he was, if not indestructible, as sharp in the ring as he'd ever been. He had been parlaying a string of good days into a gig that put the lie to the reports of TB. Back home, Herford said he could referee any time he cared to. And Jack Johnson was thinking of him as a trainer.

Gans felt so well one day that he went to New York and posted $1,000 in forfeit money to fight the new lightweight champion, Ad Wolgast, who had just beaten Nelson in a bloodbath—with both eyes battered shut in the fortieth round, Nelson imagined that he saw Wolgast in front of him when the shadow he saw was a ring post. Knowing he could make no money fighting Gans, and that reports on his health were more than the former champion had admitted, Wolgast ignored Gans's overtures. So did every other lightweight.

Gans caught another heavy cold, went back to Baltimore, and went to bed. What came of his New York visit was his impression of Jim Jeffries. Gans watched Jeffries give an exhibition in a theater and saw a fat, slow fighter who had not fought competitively in five and a half years. He would have no chance against Jack Johnson.

Tom McCarey, who knew Johnson's capabilities from having promoted several of his early fights in Los Angeles, predicted an overwhelming victory for Johnson. "He is simply a bigger edition of Joe Gans. He is the most wonderful blocker in the world, and therein lies his strength. It is next to impossible to hit him."

In a letter to Ben Selig in April 1910, Gans said he planned to attend the big heavyweight title fight and admitted—truthfully, for the first time—that he was done fighting. "Jeffries was a world-beater in his time," Gans wrote, "but his day has passed just like mine has."

•

On May 9, 1910, Gans publicly confessed his illness: He had consumption, and the disease had taken hold. That evening, he met with a reporter from the Baltimore *Sun* in the quiet outside the Goldfield. Gans said that a doctor had told him he had TB, and that on the doctor's advice he would go to Arizona in hope that the dry desert climate would help him.

Gans had trouble speaking. He coughed repeatedly and had to spit often. A friend who stood alongside gave him a small bit of whiskey mixed with rock candy syrup.

"I am a sick man," Gans told the reporter. "My trouble is tuberculosis, which in the right lung is pronounced . . . When not in training, I should weigh 140 pounds. I have lost flesh so rapidly in a few weeks that I now weigh less than 125 pounds. I sleep fairly well, but I cannot get an appetite—I can't eat at all."

Nelson was in town giving boxing exhibitions as part of a vaudeville show at the Gayety Theater on East Baltimore Street, and Gans went to see him. The two had been saying flattering things about each other in the press, and now they ended up onstage continuing their mutual praise. Gans was happy to act as referee for Nelson's sparring session. Nelson recommended a doctor he knew in Phoenix and some acquaintances Gans might visit. They parted friends, which seemed to please Gans.

The next evening, he left Baltimore by train for Arizona.

39

In the saloons and hotel lobbies of Phoenix, men talked about Joe Gans being in town and battling tuberculosis. Few supposed him to be as sick as he was. Theater managers invited him to speak to their audiences about boxing in general and the upcoming Johnson-Jeffries heavyweight championship fight in particular, but he had to decline because the disease had robbed him of his voice—time in the sun would help him regain the ability to speak normally.

He agreed to one request. The *Arizona Democrat* asked him to dictate the story of his life to a reporter. The newspaper planned ten articles and soon announced in its pages that a series by Joe Gans would appear. He believed that talking boxing with a reporter would raise his spirits, and it did, although the reporter and others who saw him found his appearance distressing. He was so thin it was difficult imagining him as lightweight champion only two years earlier.

One writer described him as "next to Sam Langford, the most gentlemanly of all pugs of color . . . Joe Gans is one of the few, the very few, in the pugilistic world, that one can really like. He is entirely different from the Jack Johnson type. Johnson is big, burly, insulting, and has an inflated idea of his own importance. Joe Gans is just the opposite."

Grantland Rice, reflecting his Southern upbringing, wrote even more disparagingly of Johnson, barging to the forefront of white America's hatred of the new heavyweight champion. William A. Harper wrote in a biography, *How You Played the Game: The Life of Grantland Rice,* that Rice disliked Johnson not only because he was the wrong color, but because he had heard about Johnson's "high-living, flashy-dressing, white-womanizing, and otherwise swaggering nature." He quoted Rice saying that Gans "knew his place" and calling him "the whitest black man that ever entered the ring, and a good bit whiter than some of the whites in that profession"—a characterization that Gans never sought but didn't object to, considering it a compliment to him and his race.

"The Smoke is of the lowest possible type of humanity—ignorant and vicious," Harper quotes Rice's opinion of Johnson. "The ethics of the sport mean about as much to him as they would to a piebald gorilla, two days out of the jungle." Rice believed "a good white man can beat a good black man seven days in the week and have something left on the side."

Gans told the Arizona reporters that Johnson would successfully defend his title in part because Jeffries hadn't fought for years. While Jeffries was a 10 to 7 favorite as the "Great White Hope," Gans warned that it would be foolish to bet on him because of his race.

"A great many people say to themselves, 'Oh, Johnson hasn't a chance to win; Jeff will kill him,'" Gans said. "Now if these same people would stop to analyze their minds, they would find that their opinion was simply the result of race prejudice. For that reason I say to the betting public, don't allow your sympathies or your race prejudice to run away with you."

"Joe Gans Tells His Life Story," the first article in a series, appeared May 23 in the *Arizona Democrat.* The first chapters recounted several of his early fights but avoided anything pertaining to race or controversy, such as the battles royal at the beginning of his career or Al Herford's manipulation of his fight with Young Griffo. The series continued in that vein. In chapter five, Gans outlined his advance toward a title fight, to which the newspaper appended a promotional paragraph: "In the next chapter of his story Gans will tell of his fight with Frank Erne for the championship. It is the best chapter yet."

Chapter six never appeared.

The June heat in Phoenix weakened Gans to the point that he could not continue the series. Nor could he do much of anything else. He stayed in bed and grew weaker. A local doctor, A. B. Hawley, recommended that he go to a higher altitude where the temperature would be cooler. On June 8, the *Democrat*, without mentioning the series' abrupt ending, reported that Gans's illness would take him that evening to Prescott, one hundred miles to the north and more than four thousand feet higher than Phoenix. It was a place known for treating TB patients.

Martha Gans lamented the lost time in Phoenix after learning of Prescott's possibilities. As it happened, Gans's train had stopped in Prescott more than three weeks earlier. Gans had marveled over the weather after stepping onto the station platform. He told a reporter who was there to greet him, referring to his lungs: "My breathing apparatus has taken the count of seven," but that a count of seven was "far from ten." "I'll be in the runnin' when a lot of you husky and ruddy-cheeked fellows are having Chopin's funeral march played for you." Climbing aboard the train to Phoenix, he had said from the steps: "You all have a fine climate. Maybe I'll come up and spend the summer."

Unexpectedly, there he was. Eliza Evans, an African American who lived on North Virginia Street in a working-class neighborhood of Prescott, took in Gans and his wife. Harry T. Southworth, Prescott's most prominent doctor, accepted Gans as a patient. The patient wasn't nearly as vigorous as he had been the day he passed through. He rarely got out of bed.

One day, he managed to write a letter to Madge, now remarried and living in Chicago. He told her of his ordeal. He wanted to make peace with her, as he had with Battling Nelson, and asked if he could see her during a stopover in Chicago whenever he went back East.

Late in June, he felt stronger. He spent much of one day walking, the first time in Prescott he had been out of bed for more than a few minutes. His appetite returned. But during the next several days, his strength waned. His appetite disappeared again and he spent most of the time indoors. Sam Langford came to visit.

On the day of the Johnson-Jeffries fight, July 4, all Gans could think of was that he should have been in Reno. For Johnson, it was a day of triumph, as he dominated Jeffries and knocked him out in the fifteenth round.

For Harry C. Carr of the *Los Angeles Times*, who had covered the Goldfield fight and defended the defeated Nelson, it was time to report the truth, but not before a couple of imaginative sentences: "I never saw any human soul so shaken with fear. When the fight began Johnson was so frightened that his face was a deadly, ashen gray. His lips were dry and his eyes were staring with a sort of horrified terror."

The fight's outcome only heightened whites' obsession with having Johnson punished—eventually he was convicted of transporting a woman across state lines "for immoral purposes" and served almost a year in prison. Whites, preoccupied with thoughts of Johnson, began to forget about Gans and his accomplishments.

Little more than two months into his trip to Arizona, Gans could not even stand, and Southworth told him not to try. A few days later, the doctor gave him worse news: He had no hope of surviving.

40

Joe Gans wanted to die at his foster mother's home in Baltimore. He offered Dr. Southworth $500 to accompany him on a train across the country. Traveling back and forth would take Southworth at least ten days away from his other patients, but he believed he would return sooner because he doubted that Gans could make it all the way. He doubted that Gans could make it very far at all.

On the evening of August 1, Gans was carried by stretcher and placed aboard a train that headed fifty miles north to Prescott Junction, where the through trains stopped. For someone in his condition, being transported to the Junction was an ordeal in itself. Just after midnight, the Santa Fe No. 4 steamed into the junction station. The writer Jim Tully was aboard.

"I was going eastward on the Santa Fe," Tully said,

and away out in the hot Arizona desert the train stopped. I got out. There were half a dozen men with a stretcher. On the stretcher was a man who was either dead or dying. He looked like a mummy—yellow parchment skin drawn tight over his bones. He didn't move. I couldn't see him breathe.

"This is a rich negro to have you fellows carrying him," I said to one of the men.

"He's not rich—he's poor," the man said. "Don't you know him? That's Joe Gans. He wants to die at home, and we're putting him on the train."

Tully knew Gans slightly. They had met in Chicago when Tully was trying to become a boxer, and Gans had given him a few tips. But after a journeyman knocked him out, Tully had turned to writing. Now, at Prescott Junction, Gans could only whisper a parting to reporters:

"I know I'm going to die, boys, and I probably will not live to come back here. I might even die before I get home, but I am going to try to hold together long enough to get to Baltimore and see mother and the two children before I cash in. Good-bye. Good luck to you. You have been awfully good to me."

Gans's wife and Kid North and Southworth, who brought an oxygen tank, accompanied him. The doctor took a seat at Gans's side in a Pullman and several times took his pulse. He found it low, and he expressed his fears to Martha Gans.

At 5:50 p.m., the train stopped at Albuquerque. A crowd had gathered, hoping to see Gans during a forty-minute stop. But he was too weak to speak. Martha did the talking.

"He realizes that he has only a short time to live. But he is the same game old Joe Gans that he always was. He is fighting the consumption just as gamely as he ever fought in the ring . . . He gained for a while in Phoenix and Prescott, but for the last few weeks he has steadily grown weaker. Last week he began to lose strength more rapidly and, knowing that death was inevitable, asked to be taken home to Baltimore to die."

That evening, the train climbed into the mountains and across the Raton Pass, which separates New Mexico and Colorado. That part of the journey, in the thin air of 7,834 feet, almost killed Gans. Southworth kept him alive with the oxygen he had brought.

At Trinidad, Colorado, a porter from another train, an admirer of Gans, boarded the No. 4. It was early morning, August 3, still dark outside. But as had occurred at Albuquerque, people gathered to get a glimpse of Gans. Shortly, the porter stepped back onto the platform and told everyone about his hero's helpless condition.

A reporter for *The Trinidad Chronicle-News* wrote: "Silent and motionless Gans lay passively looking out of the window at the landscape over which he passes, reviewing the days that are forever gone when he was the idol of his race, the undisputed champion of the lightweight class. Those were days when men became rich betting on him, days when the cities and towns opened wide their gates to welcome him, forgetful of his color. Broken in health, the mere skeleton of Gans passed through here on his way home."

Eighty miles farther, with the train stopped at La Junta, Colorado, Gans managed to speak to an Associated Press reporter. "I'm going fast," Gans told him. "I won't take my chances by stopping in Chicago." He had given up hope of seeing Madge. But during a stop in Kansas City, Missouri, he changed his mind and asked that a telegram be sent to her. They would arrive in Chicago in the morning. Would she meet the train?

And so at 11:59 a.m. on August 4, a Thursday, the Santa Fe pulled into Dearborn Street Station. People customarily gathered there to meet trains coming in from the west, and now a great crowd filled the building to welcome Gans. An acquaintance of his, John Seymour, who had taken charge of the reception, said: "I have had over a hundred requests from persons, white and black, asking me if they could do something for Joe."

The mood was festive. Old boxers laughed and talked about Gans's fights, and they expected him to join in the conversation. People knew he was sick, but they cheered at the sight of a porter, a big man, who appeared on the steps of the train. They thought Gans would be right behind him. But the man lifted his hand for quiet, and as passengers filed away solemnly from the train, it began to dawn on the waiting crowd how sick Gans was. A woman who had been on the train shouted: "Oh, let me out quick. I don't want to see a man die."

Madge, standing at the edge of the crowd, overheard the frightened woman's remark. "Is it as bad as that?" she asked.

A stretcher, with Gans on it, was passed through a window of the train. For a moment, the stretcher was held high, above the heads of the people. Then men began carrying him through the crowd. It was hot and people pushed forward to catch a glimpse of "the Old Master," but all they could see was a pinched face against a pillow. He was covered with a blanket. A gray cap had been placed on his head to shield his eyes.

"Glad to see you, boys," Gans said to some reporters. "I'm tired."

He closed his eyes.

He did not see Madge as he was carried along, but the latest Mrs. Gans did. With a few words, the current wife and the former wife greeted each other in an odd moment. Martha, dressed as elegantly as she was for Gans's fights, wore a silk dress and a hat straight from Paris; a porter carried suitcases marked with her initials. When she was a Harlem showgirl and Gans's love, Madge had looked just as glamorous, but on that day she wore a simple cotton dress and sailor hat.

"Where's Madge?" Gans asked as the men who had carried him through the station and outside along the sidewalk placed him in an ambulance.

She had hesitated when Martha Gans and the doctor had gotten into the vehicle, but Kid North motioned her inside. They were bound for her home, 3402 Wabash Avenue on the South Side. There, Gans was carried inside to where a bed had been placed in a darkened front parlor of the brick house. The women hoped the rest would revive him. Southworth didn't think it would. "Too bad his mother was not here to meet him," he said. "The odds are a thousand to one against his ever reaching his old home alive."

41

Gans rested into the afternoon, and as far as anyone could tell there was little life left in his body. At length he awakened.

"I'm going. I must go home," he said.

The women, the doctor, and Kid North all tried to talk him into staying, but he insisted.

Martha Gans made reservations on a Pennsylvania train scheduled to leave Chicago at 5:30. It would arrive in Baltimore at 3:20 the next afternoon, a Friday. Outside Madge's house, people gathered for some word from Gans, or some word about him. Martha told them that the doctor had yielded to Gans's plea to reach home and that "a start would be made to please the patient."

At five o'clock, Gans was lifted into another ambulance.

To Kid North, Gans whispered: "Kid, going home with me?"

Throughout the last leg of his journey, aboard the Pennsylvania train, the Associated Press sent bulletins on his condition. In the middle of the night, the train stopped in Crestline, Ohio, and the wire service put out the word that he was still alive. It did the same from Pittsburgh the next morning. On August 5, at 3:20 p.m., the train arrived on time at Baltimore's Union Station, where hundreds had gathered. Once more Gans was carried on a stretcher from a Pullman car to an ambulance.

He was taken to 1026 Argyle Avenue, the row house he had bought several years earlier for his foster mother. As Madge had in Chicago, Maria Gans had prepared a room for him.

•

That Sunday, Gans sent for an attorney and had papers drawn up turning over most his property to his wife and some money to his foster mother. In the three years he had managed himself, he had kept most of his money. His estate was worth about $70,000, the equivalent of about $1.6 million a century later. That was much less than he had squandered and Al Herford had taken—after his final fight, Gans estimated that he had earned more than $300,000 from boxing, the equivalent of about $7 million today.

A Baltimore doctor, John G. Jay, joined Southworth in making him comfortable. The Reverend Carroll G. Cummings of the Whatcoat Methodist Episcopal Church ministered to him; Gans sang softly, "I am so glad that Jesus loves me."

Herford visited every day. But when he left the Argyle Avenue home on August 9, he told friends that, for the first time, Gans had failed to recognize him.

Early the next morning, Southworth came to say goodbye. He was returning to Arizona. Gans managed a smile. Shortly after that, he motioned his friend Kid North to him. It was about 7:35 a.m. "Kid, Martha will teach you how . . ." With that, he suffered a coughing spell and lapsed into unconsciousness.

Gans's wife, Martha; two children, James and Julia; his foster mother, Maria; the boarder whom Gans called his uncle, William Pennington; Kid North; and a nurse were with him when he died. It was 8:08 a.m., August 10, 1910, a Wednesday. He weighed 84 pounds.

•

Al Herford told a story about Gans. Herford could have made it up. But the story rings true. The two were coming back to Baltimore by train after Gans had won the lightweight championship with his first-round knockout of Frank Erne at Fort Erie,

Ontario. They had received a number of congratulatory telegrams, including word that Gans would be honored by a great crowd at the station, with a band present and a parade to follow, and a dinner that evening.

As our train neared Baltimore, Joe and I were seated opposite each other in a parlor car. Joe was wrapped in deep silence, his sad expression even more doleful than usual.

"Isn't it wonderful, Joe," I asked, "being champion and all that it means? To have all of those folks enthused about you, and all of the money you are going to make? I'll bet your mother is proud of you."

Joe didn't say anything for a long moment. Then he said wistfully, "Yes, Mr. Herford, it sure is wonderful. But do you know what I'm thinking?"

"What?" I asked.

"That I'd give it all up—the money, the fuss, the championship, everything—for just one thing."

"What's that?" I asked.

"For a white boy's chance in the world."

42

Eubie Blake and his wife, Avis, were in Atlantic City, where he was working, when they found out Gans had died and when the burial would take place. Blake did not want to attend the funeral. He still held a grudge against Gans from their argument years before, when they had competed for the same woman.

"If you go to work and don't go to that funeral, when you come home I won't be here," Avis told Eubie. So Blake took a train to Baltimore. By the time he approached the Whatcoat Methodist Episcopal Church at Franklin and Pine streets, however, he could barely see the church through the crowd; he could not get closer than a city block.

It was August 13, a Saturday. About five thousand people, blacks and whites, hoped to get inside for the 1:00 p.m. ceremony, but most would be relegated to the streets. People cried. They cried the previous evening outside Maria Gans's home and when they passed through the parlor to view the body. From seven to ten that evening, five to seven thousand had crammed Argyle Avenue. Police kept a line intact and ushered people inside. An older woman, stooped with age, was escorted forward. The body lay in a white-silk-lined casket. The house was hot and resembled a florist's shop; flower arrangements came from as far as Seattle.

Some people left money to buy still more flowers. A man said that Gans had befriended him when he was penniless. Another who said he had traveled from New York gave ten dollars. Someone had stacked telegrams on a table. Sam Langford's was among them. And Jack Johnson's.

At 8:00 a.m., the Reverend Carroll Cummings led prayers at the house, and then the body was taken to the church. For the next four hours, mourners inched up the center aisle and paused at the casket. At noon, the doors of the church were closed. Fifteen hundred were inside.

Workers at the Goldfield—they had hung crape on the hotel's front door—sent a five-foot-high floral design of a clock with its hands pointing to the hour and minute of Gans's death. Placed near the bier, the timepiece of roses and lilies read 8:08.

Three ministers conducted the service. Lloyd Gibbs, a tenor, and Nelson Tunstall, a baritone, came down from New York and sang a number of hymns. Tunstall sang one that Gans liked, "Jesus, Lover of My Soul." Al Herford and Caleb Bond were among the honorary pallbearers. Black men from the neighborhood carried the coffin.

Outside the church, the crowd was so thick that the horse-drawn hearse could not get through. The pallbearers carried the coffin down Franklin Street to Paca Street, then right to Lexington Street, where the hearse was parked. The procession headed to the south edge of the city, to the African American cemetery, Mount Auburn. It was the largest funeral procession for a black in the city's history: one hundred and four horse-drawn carriages and three large wagons carrying flowers.

Philip Taylor, a black man, wanted to have been there. He wanted to have been part of the crowd that walked to Mount Auburn, to the plot just inside the main gate where, in years to come, Maria Gans would place flowers and champions from Benny Leonard to Mike Tyson would visit. But Taylor was locked up in a downtown police station. Police had arrested him outside the church for selling souvenirs, small Gans buttons that people could pin on their clothing, without a license.

He told the officers that he had forgotten to get a license, and apologized. It didn't amount to a lot of money, but in any case the money was not for him, he pleaded. He had been raising money for the church. They took him away anyway.

•

A few years later, Ernest Hemingway, just a teenager on his high school literary magazine in Oak Park, Illinois, wrote about Gans, awkwardly, as a high school junior might. But Gans was in the boy's imagination. In a short story titled "A Matter of Colour," a large man standing behind a curtain close to the ring hits Gans's white opponent over the head and knocks him out instead of hitting Gans—because the man with the club was color-blind.

Mahonri Young, grandson of Brigham Young, sculpted a figure of Gans. It was placed in the lobby of the Madison Square Garden on Eighth Avenue between Forty-ninth and Fiftieth Street in New York, and fighters on their way inside touched the extended left glove for luck. The statue is in the descendant of that Garden, too, but out of the way.

Gans made it into *Songs of Yale*, in the lyrics to "George Jones," a harmony about a man trying to decide the name of his firstborn son:

Gonna name him George . . . George Washington,
Christopher Columbus, Madison, and Douglas Lee . . .
Gonna name him Jim . . . Jim Jeffries, Joe Gans, Jack
Johnson, ring in a Booker T . . .

The son becomes Abe Lincoln Jones.

Archie Moore, the former light heavyweight champion, said he was a "pest" about Gans. "I could listen to grown-ups talk about him for hours and read everything I could get my hands on that mentioned him. Gans's fight with Nelson stayed with me all my life."

Sixty-seven boxers, maybe more, took the name Joe Gans. They all wanted to *be* Joe Gans.

Billie Holiday came along and, for a time growing up, lived on the same out-of-the-way Baltimore street where Joe Gans had lived, and when she sang the blues there were people who thought she was singing with Joe Gans in mind.

EPILOGUE

On September 3, 2010, the anniversary of Gans's forty-two-rounder with Nelson, I drove from Las Vegas into the desert toward Goldfield. I wanted to see what was left of the mining camp and where exactly the fight took place, which could have been done any day. But I also wanted to watch the sun set on September 3 so I could know just how the final rounds might have looked in the fading light.

I took U.S. Highway 95, which soon narrowed to two lanes. The road passed through a land of sagebrush and carried few cars. In most places it looked as if nothing had happened in a century or more. The road climbed almost imperceptibly toward Goldfield. It passed the Southern Desert Correctional Center, the Ash Meadows National Wildlife Refuge, the Shady Lady Ranch brothel, and, unseen to the right behind mountain ranges for almost the entire 184 miles, the Nevada Test and Training Range, operated by the United States Air Force Warfare Center.

You know when you reach Goldfield. There's a green sign with the name of the place and its altitude, and the speed limit of seventy plummets to twenty-five. The highway bends sharply left, becoming Crook Avenue. Tex Rickard's little brick house is there on the left, on the corner of Franklin.

The place was almost deserted. So was the whole area. Goldfield is in a part of the country large in size and small in population, one person to every three square miles. Three whiskered men sat on wooden steps out front of the general store in what looked like a movie set. During a visit of several hours, I saw only four other people. Several houses and stores were empty; some were for rent or for sale. A sign at a gasoline station said OPEN EXCEPT WHEN CLOSED.

Bryan Smalley knew about Gans and Nelson. He's an Esmeralda County deputy sheriff, and "ten or fifteen years ago" he had placed a marker on the spot where the fight was held. A pleasant man perhaps in his fifties, he led the way to the fight site in his white police car, traveling over unpaved Miners Avenue and past Fourth Street until there were no more street signs. He parked in the dust. We walked a few feet uphill on gray sand strewn with stones until we came to flat ground. There, an aluminum plate affixed to a large rock read: LOCATION OF GANS-NELSON FIGHT, 1906.

We stood in the middle of an automotive junkyard. The vehicles were skeletons. One was burned to rust, and all had been stripped of their engines and other innards. Even most of the chrome that could identify the brand of car or truck or trailer or motor home had been taken, although one car had almost all its letters: ORD. Smalley said that people around there—and there were about 220—"needed parts."

The cemetery that had been close to where the fight had taken place was gone; Smalley said that years before, in the middle of a night, the bodies had been exhumed and buried farther out of town.

Columbia Mountain, where two prospectors found gold in 1902, setting off the rush, towered about a mile to the northeast. Then, and in the years that followed, you could scoop gold off the topsoil with your cupped hand. But whereas homes and tents once stretched all the way to the mountain's base from Crook Avenue, now there was only scrubland interrupted mostly by falling-down shacks, some nailed shut, and foundations of missing buildings. Like boxing's greats, almost everyone had vanished.

Everything comes to dust, prizefights in mining camps, crowds of 125,000 jammed into wooden stadiums, Friday nights in the Garden, closed-circuit TV fights beamed into theaters and hotel ballrooms, except every once in a while, in the dust, there is some hint, maybe two reels of a fight film, unsteady but undeniably defining, when on the surface of something as plain as the middle of the desert, nothing is apparent.

NOTES ON SOURCES: THE RESEARCH

SELECTED BIBLIOGRAPHY

ACKNOWLEDGMENTS

INDEX

NOTES ON SOURCES:
THE RESEARCH

I first thought of writing about Joe Gans in 2003 and started pursuing him—pursuing in the sense of research and note-taking—in 2004. This was a departure for me. Having spent thirty-nine years on staff at *The Washington Post* and two more years there as a part-time writer, I was more familiar with press boxes than libraries. I began work on Gans at the Library of Congress with a one-evening class on the vastness and complexities of the place, from which I took this advice: If returning, bring patience. Often the research was slow going. But I found that repeated visits there and work at other libraries proved as instructive, and satisfying, as most of my journeys as a newspaperman.

I did research at the Enoch Pratt Free Library, the Maryland Historical Society, and the Reginald F. Lewis Museum of Maryland African American History and Culture, all in Baltimore, and at the Maryland State Archives, in Annapolis; in Nevada, at the Lied Library at the University of Nevada at Las Vegas, the Nevada State Museum in Carson City, and the Central Nevada Museum in Tonopah; in California, at the LA84 Foundation, the Huntington Library in San Marino, the Arcadia Historical Museum, the Arcadia Public Library, and the San Francisco Public Library; and at the University of Maryland's Hornbake Library, the Frost Library at Amherst College, and the Samuel L. Paley Library at Temple University. Ryan Flahive and Scott Anderson at the Sharlot Hall Museum in Prescott, Arizona, and Laura Palma-Blandford at the Arizona State Archives in Phoenix helped with the research. I made it to Goldfield.

Had Abraham Lincoln lived a little longer, his life and Gans's would have overlapped. But there were relatives, sportswriters, and historians to provide information. I am indebted for interviews to Arlene Maxwell, her sisters Lois Shields and Emelda Custis, and her mother, Mary Brown, all related to Gans; the historian Hank Kaplan, whom I visited at his home in Miami in July 2006; Michael Katz and Al Goldstein, two admirable boxing writers; Bob Nylen, Curator of History at the Nevada State Museum in Carson City, and Angela Haag, researcher at the Central Nevada Museum in Tonopah; Bryan Smalley, who took me to the site of Gans's forty-two-rounder and provided some of Goldfield's history; and Daun van Ee, specialist in twentieth-century American history at the Library of Congress.

The Library of Congress proved to be the best place to learn about Gans, as it is, of course, the best place to learn about countless other people and subjects. I am grateful to Dave Kelly, a librarian there who helped me immensely; David Smith, who did the same at the New York Public Library, and at whose suggestion I visited the library's Schomburg Center for Research in Black Culture; and Tony Cucchiara of Brooklyn College's library, which obtained the Hank Kaplan boxing collection after Hank's death in 2007 and established the Hank Kaplan Boxing Archive. All three—Kelly, Smith, and Cucchiara—knew boxing and Gans's place in its history.

Dave Kelly suggested to me the Library of Congress website, loc.gov, where I accessed its historic newspapers digital collection. Much of the information on Gans that I found helpful came from *The San Francisco Call, The Salt Lake Herald*, the *Los Angeles Herald*, the New York *World*, and *The Washington Times*. Since the notes that follow are intended as a general guide to my research, I have included the date from those newspapers, and from other publications, only when I found the material to be important to the story.

In addition to the newspapers on the Library of Congress website, others that were helpful were *The Afro-American Ledger, The* (Baltimore) *Sun, The Boston Daily Globe, The Chicago Defender*, the *Chicago Daily Tribune, The Goldfield Daily Sun, The New York Times*, and the *San Francisco Examiner*. I referred to at least forty-one other newspapers, many accessed through loc .gov and newspaperarchive.com. Ancestry.com was also helpful. So were online articles by Monte D. Cox, including "Joe Gans, the Old Master: Was He The Greatest of Them All?" In addition, I consulted a number of magazines, including *Boxing Illustrated Wrestling News, Esquire, Everybody's Magazine, Nevada Magazine, The New Yorker*, and *The Ring*.

For the Gans-Nelson fight at Goldfield, I relied on the Associated Press's round-by-round account, which appeared in many newspapers, and the film of the fight, which is available to be viewed at the Library of Congress.

I was the beneficiary of several writers and researchers who came before me, but above all there was Sally Zanjani, whose work on early Nevada I discovered in the main reading room of the Thomas Jefferson Building at the Library of Congress. She brought Goldfield alive, and Gans, too, when he was there, and I was able to begin Gans's story the way I wanted to largely because of two of her books, *Goldfield: The Last Gold Rush on the Western Frontier* and *The Glory Days in Goldfield, Nevada*. Another book that was helpful was Charles Samuels's *The Magnificent Rube: The Life and Gaudy Times of Tex Rickard*.

ONE

That Gans was fighting for the 187th time is based on the records of BoxRec
.com. On page 24 of *Goldfield*, Zanjani explains the naming of the place. Jack
London called Battling Nelson "the abysmal brute" in the *San Francisco Examiner* of September 10, 1905. Walt Whitman's quote comes from his *Democratic Vistas*, originally published in 1871. Al Herford's manipulation of Gans
was described in many places.

TWO

Zanjani writes about the difficult trip to Goldfield on page 31 of *Goldfield* and
pages 11–13 of *The Glory Days in Goldfield, Nevada*. If it weren't for *Goldfield*, I wouldn't have known that a visitor likened the place to "Dante's Inferno with the lid off" (page 75), or that another found it to be a place "where
the desolations meet" (page 73). On page 166 of *Goldfield*, Zanjani identifies
Parmeter Kent as Sidney Flower, the magazine publisher who had been shut
down for mail fraud in Chicago. On page 46 of *The Glory Days in Goldfield,
Nevada*, she cites a rush of people from around the world to the mining camp.
Carl B. Glasscock's *Gold in Them Hills: The Story of the West's Last Wild
Mining Days*, page 219, and *The Goldfield Daily Sun* provide details of the
camp and people hurrying to get there. *The Goldfield Daily Sun*, "Gans First
to Be on the Scene," August 8, 1906, covers Gans's arrival in Goldfield on the
evening of August 7. Samuels's *The Magnificent Rube*, pages 102–104, refers
to Larry Sullivan, his management of a sailors' rooming house in Seattle, his
notoriety and his nickname, and his conversations with Gans.

THREE

The Magnificent Rube covers the mourning for Rickard at his death with a
photograph and a caption before page 151, and also provides details of Rickard's background, his exploits in the Yukon and Alaska, his rush to Goldfield,
and his role in settling on Gans and Nelson as the fighters. Samuels describes
the Northern saloon's interior on page 93 of *The Magnificent Rube*. John
L. (Ike) Dorgan's article in *The Ring* of August 1928, "Once Gambler, Always
Gambler, True of 'Tex' Rickard," provides details. That Goldfield had fifty-
three saloons is in the *Los Angeles Times*, "The Rush Was On: On Sept. 3,
1906, in Goldfield, Nev., Two Lightweights Struck It Rich," June 12, 1988.
The Goldfield Athletic Club's formation occurred July 30, 1906, and was reported that day by *The Goldfield Daily Sun* and daily thereafter in "Calendar
of Events Leading Up to the Fight," and in Glasscock's *Gold in Them Hills*,
pages 226–27. Phillip I. Earl explains Rickard's demeanor and attire in
"King of the Matchmakers" in *Nevada Magazine*, September/October 1980.

Samuels reports on Rickard's telegram to Joe Humphreys and Humphreys's response on pages 89–90 of *The Magnificent Rube*. Geoffrey C. Ward notes Rickard's belief that he could "sell" the Goldfield fight "as a struggle for racial superiority" on page 169 of *Unforgivable Blackness: The Rise and Fall of Jack Johnson*. An exchange of telegrams between Rickard and Nolan/Nelson are in Nelson's autobiography, *Battling Nelson: His Life, Battles and Career*, page 201, and in a page 1 box, untitled, in *The Goldfield Daily Sun* of August 3, 1906. George Graham Rice as a pseudonym is on page 9 of the introduction to the new edition of Rice's *My Adventures with Your Money*. Samuels mentions "the Jackal of Wall Street" on page 103 of *The Magnificent Rube*. Wingfield and Nixon organizing the Goldfield Consolidated Mines Company is on page 52 of Zanjani's *Goldfield*. Baruch and Frick are referred to in an article by C. Elizabeth Raymond, "George Wingfield's Political Machine: A Study in Historical Reputation," which is included in the book *Nevada: Readings and Perspectives*, edited by Michael S. Green and Gary E. Elliott. Samuels, in *The Magnificent Rube*, page 101, relates that Rickard had stacks of gold pieces exhibited at the bank. *The Goldfield Daily Sun* of August 7, 1906, mentions Rickard's trip to Reno and repeats it daily thereafter in "Calendar of Events Leading Up to the Fight."

FOUR

Many newspapers covered the split of the purse and other demands by Nelson's manager, Billy Nolan; George Siler, the *Chicago Daily Tribune*'s sports editor who would referee the Goldfield fight, wrote a column that ran August 31, 1906, "Nolan Acts the Role of Tyrant." Samuels's *The Magnificent Rube* also includes a discussion of the purse on page 101. Gans's quote "I'll weigh in harness" is in *The Goldfield Daily Sun* of August 29, 1906. His quote "I could fight on top of a Saratoga trunk" is in *The Washington Times* of September 8, 1907.

FIVE

Lawrence T. Carter cites the incident at the trolley stop on pages 39–40 of *Eubie Blake: Keys of Memory*. The *New York American*'s article "Gans, Greatest of Fighters, a Negro?" was published on December 22, 1907.

SIX

Zanjani describes the inside of Rickard's saloon on page 80 of *Goldfield*. "Typical" apparel of the card players is described in *A Lady in Boomtown: Miners and Manners on the Nevada Frontier*, by Mrs. Hugh Brown. The town's crowds and discomforts are apparent in photographs throughout Zanjani's *The Glory Days in Goldfield, Nevada.* The reference to "Sadie, Sylvia, Jessie . . ." comes from a photo on page 75. On page 96, Zanjani includes a quote beginning "Most of the men wear guns," which she attributes to an earlier writer. Zanjani mentions opium dens on page 137 of *Goldfield.* Glasscock's *Gold in Them Hills,* page 158, extols the Palm Grill. Rickard's home is described by Samuels on pages 113–14 of *The Magnificent Rube,* and Zanjani on pages 62–63 of *The Glory Days in Goldfield, Nevada.* Zanjani mentions Rickard's car on page 134 of *Goldfield.* A quote about Rickard, "luck gave him the cards . . . ," is on page 296 of *The Magnificent Rube.*

SEVEN

Gans settling in at the Merchants Hotel is from "Nelson Gets Quarters," an article in *The Goldfield Daily Sun* of August 17, 1906. The poker game is noted in "Goldfield Has Gone Fight Mad" in *The Salt Lake Herald* of September 2, 1906. Rex Beach's quote is from an article he did for *Everybody's Magazine* in April 1907 titled "The Fight at Tonopah." Gans's conversation with John Sparks is in *The San Francisco Call* of August 18, 1906, in "George Siler Chosen to Referee the Gans-Nelson Fight at Goldfield." *The Goldfield Daily Sun,* "Gans Takes Things Luxuriously," August 13, 1906, reports on trainer Frank McDonald's arrival on the evening of August 12.

EIGHT

Information on Martha Davis comes mostly from the Baltimore *Sun,* especially "Gans Wins This Fight," October 2, 1908. Death certificates of Gans's children James and Julia at the Maryland State Archives suggest that both were born to Gans's first wife. An October 18, 1959, article in *The Sun's Sunday* magazine, "Greatest Lightweight Who Ever Lived," says the children were by Gans's first wife. A *Baltimore Morning Herald* article of February 10, 1900, says that Gans's eight-year-old son attended a bout in New York in 1900. Gan's descendants, especially his great-granddaughter Arlene Maxwell, as well as research at the Maryland State Archives, provided the information on Gertrude Gans. Gans's first two marriages are on record at the Maryland State Archives. The Baltimore *Sun* reported Gans's and his third wife's divorce attempts.

NINE

Ellison's description of a battle royal is on page 22 of the Second Vintage International Edition of *Invisible Man.* The Mencken quote comes from *The New Yorker,* April 25, 1942, in an article beginning on page 18 called "Days of Innocence: Master of Gladiators." On page 39 of *Eubie Blake*, Carter says Gans's real name was Josephus Butts. Baltimore newspapers reported Gans's original last name as Butts, his adoption, and, sketchily, his early life. The Baltimore *Sun* reported on Gans's encounter with James Kernan, Kernan's hotel, and Gans's bout witnessed by his "uncle."

TEN
The material on Herford and the young Gans can be found in the Baltimore *Sun*. *The Baltimore News* of August 11, 1910, in "Gans' First Fight Was in a Parlor, Old-Timer Writes," printed an account of Gans's bout with the "trial horse." The Ned Beaumont quote is from his book *The Savage Science of Streetfighting: Applying the Lessons of Championship Boxing to Serious Street Survival*, page 75. The prank Gans played on Kid North is in Carter's *Eubie Blake*, pages 40–41.

ELEVEN
Much of the Caruso material comes from *Enrico Caruso*, by Pierre V. A. Key with Bruno Zirato, and *The San Francisco Calamity: Told by Eye Witnesses*, edited by Charles Morris. The Baltimore *Sun* of April 19 and May 5, 1906, reported on Gans's experiences in San Francisco. *The Chicago Defender* of November 21, 1936, recounted Gans's meeting with Biddy Bishop. "San Francisco is gone" is in Jack London's "The Story of an Eyewitness," in the May 5, 1906, *Collier's*. *The New York Times* of May 13, 1906, had Gans among those fighting exhibition matches for the earthquake victims.

TWELVE
Dorgan coined the nickname "the Old Master" according to Monte D. Cox at coxscorner.tripod.com/interview.html. *The Goldfield Daily Sun* of August 24 and 25, 1906, included fighters picking Gans to win the forty-two-rounder. Robert Edgren, sports editor and syndicated columnist for New York's *The World*, quoted Young Corbett; the story ran in *The Boston Daily Globe* of September 1, 1906. Gans's "Oregon boot" quote is in Joel L. Priest's article "Goldfield Has Gone Fight Mad" in *The Salt Lake Herald* of September 2, 1906.

THIRTEEN
The Nelson material comes from his autobiography, *Battling Nelson: His Life, Battles and Career*; *The San Francisco Call*; Samuels's *The Magnificent Rube*;

The New York Times; The Goldfield Daily Sun; the *Chicago Daily Tribune;* and "The Battle of Goldfield," by Steven R. Nicolaisen in the September/ October 1980 issue of *Nevada Magazine.* BoxRec.com gives Nelson's birth name as Oscar Mattheus Nielson.

FOURTEEN
Gans drawing the color line was reported by Siler in the *Chicago Daily Tribune,* August 5, 1906.

FIFTEEN
Wilson Mizner's story is from "Profiles: Legend of a Sport," a July 29, 1950, *New Yorker* article by Alva Johnston, beginning on page 26 of the magazine. Nan Patterson is included in a *Sports Illustrated* article by Berne S. Jacobsen from August 5, 1968, titled "When Goldfield Was Aglitter," on page 75 of the magazine. The "fattest faro dealer" is mentioned in the Baltimore *Sun* of September 3, 1906. The George Nixon quote was in *The San Francisco Call* of August 15, 1906. "Coon fruit" was in the *Fairbanks* (Alaska) *Evening News* of September 1, 1906, under the headline "Joe Gans Is the Prime Favorite in Big Fight." The newspaper attributes the article to the Associated Press, but it misspells Goldfield in the dateline as Goldfields; the article was found on newspaperarchive.com.

SIXTEEN
The "I'll attend to you" quote from Gans is in the *Tonopah Daily Sun.* Prefight amusements are listed in a *Tonopah Times-Bonanza* article of February 12, 1954, entitled "Nelson's Death Recalls Goldfield's 'Greatest Day.'" Wodehouse used "bring home the bacon" in his short story "The Long Hole."

SEVENTEEN
Barton W. Currie, reporting from Goldfield, discusses the heat in an article he wrote on the afternoon of the fight, September 3, 1906, for the New York *World:* "It has been warm for the past two days, about 100 in the shade. It is something like 110 at the arena, so that there is no doubt but that the fighters will take off a lot of weight in the course of their festivities." Rickard's filling in the empty seats is in the *Tonopah Times-Bonanza* of February 12, 1954. Gans's refusal of tape and his selection of the southwest corner of the ring was reported by the Associated Press and included in the *Los Angeles Herald* of September 4, 1906. Information on the Miles brothers is in *The San Francisco*

Call. The description of the sheriff's deputies is in the *Los Angeles Herald* of September 4, 1906 (and other newspapers), as is the quote, "show yourself and turn your face toward the moving pictures." The fight's starting time of 3:23 p.m. is in the *Chicago Daily Tribune.*

EIGHTEEN

Monte D. Cox, in an article online at coxscorner.tripod.com/goat2.html titled "Joe Gans, the Old Master: Was He the Greatest of Them All?", mentions three-, four-, and five-punch combinations Gans threw in Goldfield. Reports on when Gans met up with Fitzsimmons vary. *The Chicago Defender* of January 23, 1937, says that Gans attended Fitzsimmons's fight in Baltimore in 1893 and began learning from him then. Fitzsimmons's background comes from several sources, including *Remembering Bob Fitzsimmons*, by William H. Rocap and Pember W. Rocap; the Dale Webb book *Prize Fighter: The Life and Times of Bob Fitzsimmons*; the Philadelphia *Bulletin*; Fitzsimmons's own *Physical Culture and Self-Defense*; and Mike Casey online at boxingscene.com/?m=show&id=6203. The Harry Lenny quote is in "This Was Joe Gans," by Johnny Brannigan, in *Boxing Illustrated Wrestling News*, August 1960.

NINETEEN

Much of the information on early films is in an online article, "The Latham Loop," at pictureshowman.com/articles_technology_latham.cfm. Some of its information is attributed to *A Million and One Nights: A History of the Motion Picture*, a 1926 work by Terry Ramsaye. *Fight Pictures: A History of Boxing and Early Cinema*, by Dan Streible, was a valuable source and an impressive example of research.

TWENTY

The material on Gans's New York fights was covered by several New York newspapers. The John Tyler Morgan quote comes from an article in the January 17, 1895, Baltimore *Sun* titled "The Negro's Natural Home." That 2,400 African Americans were hanged or burned at the stake comes from www.digitalhistory.uh.edu, from the page titled "Lynching, Period: 1880–1920." An article about the railroad construction workers who were hanged was in *The Salt Lake Herald* of November 19, 1895, under the headline "Where Human Life Is Cheap." The incident involving Thomas Hardwick was reported by *The Baltimore News* and reprinted by *The Afro-American Ledger* of March 10, 1906. John McGraw's story about Gans is on page 70 of Charles C. Alexander's *John McGraw. The Afro-American* reported on Bert Williams on August 31, 1923. The lyrics that included Gans were in the December 1944 issue of *Esquire*, in "The Old Master of the Ring."

TWENTY-ONE

Gans confesses to being unprepared for his first fight with McFadden in "The Story of My Ring Career," chapter five, which was published on June 4, 1910, by the *Arizona Democrat*. Dan Daniel writes that Gans had been hit "right in the pie" in *The Ring* of June 1960. The Citro quote comes from "Cornerman: Helping Boxers Survive the Cut," an article by Mark Stuart Gill in the December 4, 1989, *Sports Illustrated*. The material on "yellow journalism" is from Dan Streible's *Fight Pictures: A History of Boxing and Early Cinema*. Hogan's article is quoted on page 92 of *The Sweet Science Goes Sour: How Scandal Brought Boxing to Its Knees*, by Thomas Myler. The fix at Tattersall's was reported by many newspapers, the *Chicago Daily Tribune*'s accounts being the most thorough. Edgar Lee Masters wrote about Bob Fitzsimmons in "The Time of Ruby Robert," in the February 1940 *Esquire*.

TWENTY-TWO

The Fitzsimmons quote about Gans is from the *Los Angeles Times* of September 2, 1906, "Fitz Likes Black Champ." "It is not strength, but art, obtains the prize" is in Alexander Pope's translation of Homer's *Iliad*, Book XXIII, line 383. Tiger Woods's quote comes from an interview with reporters before the 2009 United States Open. Much of the Harry Lenny material is in "This Was Joe Gans," by Johnny Brannigan, in the *Boxing Illustrated Wrestling News* of August 1960, and Kelly Richard Nicholson's *Hitters, Dancers and Ring Magicians: Seven Boxers of the Golden Age and Their Challengers*. Sam Langford's quotes about Gans's measuring an opponent and likening Joe Louis to Gans are in an article titled "'Joe Louis Is Another Joe Gans'—Sam Langford" in *The Chicago Defender* of July 20, 1935. George Dixon being struck by his manager is reported in *The Boston Daily Globe* of February 6, 1892, "Dixon Angry."

TWENTY-THREE

The final punch of the fight was "a hard left half-scissors hook to the liver . . ." according to Nelson's account on page 206 of his autobiography, and many newspapers. The Picasso quote is from "Picasso and the Masters," an exhibition at the Grand Palais, Paris, 2008–2009. Gans's telegram to his foster mother is in an article titled "No Foul, Declares Nolan" in *The Washington Post* of September 5, 1906. The second telegram and Jim Casey's story are in *Big Brown: The Untold Story of UPS*, by Greg Niemann, page 40. The Atlanta

Race Riot material is from "100 Years Later, a Painful Episode Is Observed at Last" in *The New York Times* of September 24, 2006.

TWENTY-FOUR
Fred Sander's letter to his future wife, dated September 5, 1906, is in *Goldfield Remembered*, published by the Goldfield Historical Society; I came upon the book in the Central Nevada Museum at Tonopah. Gans's quote that Nelson spit in his face during the fight is in "Nelson in Bed; Gans Takes Air" in *The Washington Times* of September 5, 1906. George Graham Rice's version of the fight and its ending is on pages 122–23 of his book *My Adventures with Your Money*. George Springmeyer's shock at seeing the bruised Nelson is on page 133 of Sally Zanjani's *Goldfield*.

TWENTY-FIVE
I covered the fight in Los Angeles but was reminded of the applause Ali received by Shelby Coffey, my editor when I wrote for the Style section of *The Washington Post*.

TWENTY-SIX
The Walters quote is from *The New York Times* of October 10, 1906. Gans's claim that Nolan adjusted the fight film is in Streible's *Fight Pictures*, page 200. Cobb's salary is in Charles C. Alexander's book *Ty Cobb*, page 65. Jimmy Cannon wrote about George Barton in the *New York Post* of December 3, 1956. Information on the Milwaukee banquet and Madge Gans being in Cincinnatti is in the *Milwaukee Free Press*.

TWENTY-SEVEN
Much of the material on the Gans-Herman fight is in Rex Beach's article "The Fight at Tonopah" in *Everybody's Magazine*, April 1907, pages 464–74. Nat Fleischer, in "An Untold Story of Rickard's Career" in *The Ring* of February 1932, notes that the Bronco Kid in *The Spoilers* is modeled after Rickard. Joe Louis predicted he would knock out Max Schmeling in "The Joe Louis I Remember," by Jimmy Cannon, collected in *The Fireside Book of Boxing*, edited by W. C. Heinz. Gans's confrontation at the hotel in St. Paul is in the *La Crosse Tribune*, November 11, 1907, "Joe Gans Gets Body Blow at the Ryan."

TWENTY-EIGHT

James Jackson spoke with the distinguished reporter J. Anthony Lukas, then working for the Baltimore *Sun*; his article ran on December 6, 1960. Gans's establishment was on Chestnut Street, which is now Colvin Street. The information in this chapter comes mainly from *The Sun*, *The Afro-American Ledger*, the Carter book *Eubie Blake*, and an article by Elton C. Fax, "Incident at the Goldfield," in *Maryland* magazine, Autumn 1979. Information also comes from Al Rose's book *Eubie Blake*; the *Call and Post* in Ohio; *The San Francisco Call*; and *The Boston Daily Globe*. Information about Luckey Roberts comes from "Luckey Roberts and the Transition from Ragtime to Jazz," an article by Barry Kernfeld found at American National Biography Online.

TWENTY-NINE

This chapter is based largely on articles in *The San Francisco Call*, *The Salt Lake Herald*, and *The Washington Post*. Maria Gans's "whole hog" quote is from *The Washington Post* of September 11, 1907.

THIRTY

Material on Lucky Baldwin came from several sources, including C. B. Glasscock's *The Story of an Unconventional Success*. My research on Baldwin at the Arcadia Historical Museum and the Arcadia Public Library helped shape this chapter. The exchange between Gans and Tommy Burns was reported by Eddie Smith in *The Oakland Tribune* of July 22, 1907, in an article titled "Joe Gans Is Matched to Meet Hardy Jimmy Burns." The black spectator was described in the *Los Angeles Herald* of September 23, 1907, in an article titled "Big Crowd Watches Joe." Gans's billing as "conqueror of the white race" was included in an advertisement in the *Los Angles Herald* of September 28, 1907.

THIRTY-ONE

Information about Jimmy Dougherty was accessed at the Jimmy (Baron) Dougherty entry of the online Boxrec Boxing Encyclopaedia. The Leiperville story is recounted at eastsideboxing.com in an article by Keith Terceira called "Joe Gans: The Old Master." Zanjani's statement is on page 132 of *Goldfield*. Steven A. Riess wrote an article on Gans in *American National Biography* that mentioned Gans's tuberculosis. Tully's quotes are in "Famous Negroes of the Ring," an article in the April 1927 *Vanity Fair*.

THIRTY-TWO

The San Francisco Call was the main source for this chapter. The line from Tennyson is in his poem "Ulysses."

THIRTY-THREE

The Heinz quote is on page 135 of *The Fireside Book of Boxing*, which Heinz compiled. Much of the material in the chapter is from *The San Francisco Call*, including Rube Goldberg's sketches and his article the morning after the second Gans-Nelson fight; at the time, Goldberg was on vacation from the New York *Mail*. The Baltimore *Sun* carried reaction to Gans's defeat, especially in "Down at Joe's Hotel," July 5, 1908. The Associated Press's round-by-round account of the fight ran in many newspapers.

THIRTY-FOUR

Again, I relied on *The San Francisco Call*, and the AP's round-by-round description of the fight.

THIRTY-FIVE

The Baltimore *Sun* reported Gans's divorce July 18, 1908, and forthcoming wedding October 2, 1908.

THIRTY-SIX

Theodore Roosevelt's *An Autobiography*, page 50, contains the "stanch friend" quote. *The New York Times* published its opposition to all mixed-race bouts on November 1, 1909, in a piece titled "And May the Best Man Win!" which was part of "Topics of The Times." Charley Rose, the matchmaker, is quoted in the *The Ring* of June 1967, page 34. Charlie White's quote that Gans was finished as a fighter, carried by the AP, ran in the Baltimore *Sun* of March 30, 1909. Gans's claim of good health was in *The Chicago Defender*, "Billy Nolan Murders Joe Gans for Measly Dollar," August 6, 1910.

THIRTY-SEVEN

Most of the Bellows material comes from the Bellows papers, which I read in the Frost Library at Amherst College. Marianne Doezema's quote is from page 106 of her book *George Bellows and Urban America*, which she discussed with me, along with mixed-race bouts in general, in a telephone conversation. I visited the National Gallery of Art several times, and discussed the painting *Both Members of This Club* with curators and authorities on Bellows, either at the gallery or by phone.

THIRTY-EIGHT
The Odgen Standard carried Tom McCarey's quote about Jack Johnson in an article titled "Johnson Is Powerful" on December 7, 1909.

THIRTY-NINE
Pages 163 and 164 of *How You Played the Game: The Life of Grantland Rice,* by William A. Harper, contain Rice's quotes and feelings about Jack Johnson. The Sharlot Hall Museum and other researchers gathered material for me on Gans's days in Arizona.

FORTY
Librarians and newspaper accounts in the cities and towns along Gans's train route from Arizona to Chicago enabled me to report on his trip. Most of the quoted material from when he was in Chicago comes from *The Eau Claire* (Wisconsin) *Leader* of August 6, 1910.

FORTY-ONE
Gans's estimate that he earned $300,000 from boxing is in the *Milwaukee Evening Wisconsin* of July 16, 1909. The Baltimore *Sun* covered Gans's final days. Johnny Brannigan listed Gans's weight at death as 84 pounds in "This Was Joe Gans," in the August 1960 *Boxing Illustrated Wrestling News.* Herford's reminiscence is in the January 1963 *Negro Digest,* in an article titled "A Champion's Lost Ambition," by Harry Keck. BoxRec.com lists Gans's record as 145-10 with 16 draws, plus decisions rendered by newspapermen as 14-2 with 4 draws, plus 5 fights ruled no contest, a total of 196 bouts.

FORTY-TWO
Eubie Blake and his attendance at Gans's funeral is on page 46 of Carter's *Eubie Blake.* The Baltimore newspapers covered the scene at Maria Gans's home and the funeral. The Philip Taylor story is in *The Baltimore News* of August 13, 1910, in an article titled "Uses Gans' Funeral to Swell Church's Finances and Lands Behind Bars." The Young material is online at mag .rochester.edu/seeingAmerica/essays/50.swf. Archie Moore wrote about Gans in *The Archie Moore Story,* page 9.

SELECTED BIBLIOGRAPHY

Alexander, Charles C. *John McGraw*. Lincoln, Nebraska, and London: University of Nebraska Press, Bison Books, 1995.

———. *Ty Cobb*. New York and Oxford: Oxford University Press, 1984.

Anderson, Dave, editor. *The Red Smith Reader*. New York: Random House, 1982.

Ashe, Arthur R., Jr. *A Hard Road to Glory: A History of the African-American Athlete 1619–1918*. New York: Warner Books, An Amistad Book, 1988.

———. *A Hard Road to Glory: Boxing; the African-American Athlete in Boxing*. New York: Amistad Press, 1993.

Aycock, Colleen, and Mark Scott. *Joe Gans: A Biography of the First African American World Boxing Champion*. Jefferson, North Carolina: McFarland and Company, 2008.

Bak, Richard. *Joe Louis: The Great Black Hope*. Dallas: Taylor Publishing, 1996.

Batchelor, Denzil. *Jack Johnson and His Times*. London: Weidenfeld and Nicolson, 1990.

Beaumont, Ned. *The Savage Science of Streetfighting: Applying the Lessons of Championship Boxing to Serious Street Survival*. Boulder, Colorado: Paladin Press, 2001.

BoxRec.com.

Brown, Mrs. Hugh (Marjorie). *Lady in Boomtown: Miners and Manners on the Nevada Frontier*. Reno and Las Vegas: University of Nevada Press, 1991.

Cannon, Jack, and Tom Cannon, editors. *Nobody Asked Me, But . . . : The World of Jimmy Cannon*. New York: Holt, Rinehart and Winston, 1978.

Carter, Lawrence T. *Eubie Blake: Keys of Memory*. Detroit: Balamp, 1979.

Cavanaugh, Jack. *Tunney: Boxing's Brainiest Champ and His Upset of the Great Jack Dempsey*. New York: Ballantine, 2007.

Coxscorner.tripod.com.

Doezema, Marianne. *George Bellows and Urban America*. New Haven: Yale University Press, 1992.

Eastsideboxing.com.

Ellison, Ralph. *Invisible Man*. New York: Vintage Books, Second Vintage International Edition, 1995.

Fitzsimmons, Robert. *Physical Culture and Self-Defense*. London and Philadelphia: Drexel Biddle, 1901.

Glasscock, Carl B. *Gold in Them Hills: The Story of the West's Last Wild Mining Days*. Indianapolis: Bobbs-Merrill, 1932.

——. *The Story of an Unconventional Success*. Indianapolis: Bobbs-Merrill, 1933.

Green, Michael S., and Gary E. Elliott, editors. *Nevada Readings and Perspectives*. Reno: Nevada Historical Society, 1997.

Harper, William A. *How You Played the Game: The Life of Grantland Rice*. Columbia: University of Missouri Press, 1999.

Heinz, W. C., editor. *The Fireside Book of Boxing*. New York: Simon & Schuster, 1961.

——. *Once They Heard the Cheers*. New York: Doubleday, 1979.

Heller, Peter. *"In This Corner . . . !" Forty-two World Champions Tell Their Stories*. Cambridge, Massachusetts: Da Capo Press, Perseus Books Group, 1994.

Johnson, Jean, editor. *Boomtown History: Centennial Celebration of Nye County, Nevada, and Death Valley Area Mining Camps*. Amargosa: Nevada Boomtown History Event, 2006.

——. *Boomtown History II: Celebration of Goldfield-Tonopah Area Boomtowns*. Amargosa: Nevada Boomtown History Event, 2007.

——. *Boomtown History III: Life in Goldfield and Tonopah's Boomtowns*. Tonopah, Nevada: Boomtown History Conferences, 2009.

Johnston, J. J., and Sean Curtin. *Chicago Boxing*. Charleston, South Carolina: Arcadia, 2005.

Key, Pierre V. A., with Bruno Zirato. *Enrico Caruso*. Boston: Little, Brown, 1922.

Liebling, A. J. *The Sweet Science*. New York: Viking, 1956.

Moore, Archie. *The Archie Moore Story*. New York: McGraw-Hill, 1960.

Morris, Charles, editor. *The San Francisco Calamity: Told by Eye Witnesses*. Philadelphia: J. C. Winston Co., 1906.

Moyle, Clay. *Sam Langford: Boxing's Greatest Uncrowned Champion*. Seattle: Bennett and Hastings, 2006.

Myler, Thomas. *The Sweet Science Goes Sour: How Scandal Brought Boxing to Its Knees*. Vancouver: Greystone Books, 2006.

Nelson, Battling. *Battling Nelson: His Life, Battles and Career*. Hegewisch, Illinois: Self-published, 1908.

Nicholson, Kelly Richard. *Hitters, Dancers and Ring Magicians: Seven Boxers of the Golden Age and Their Challengers.* Jefferson, North Carolina: McFarland, 2011.

Niemann, Greg. *Big Brown: The Untold Story of UPS.* San Francisco: Jossey-Bass, a Wiley Imprint, 2007.

Oates, Joyce Carol. *On Boxing.* New York: Ecco, 2002.

Ramsaye, Terry. *A Million and One Nights: A History of the Motion Picture Through 1925.* A Touchstone Book accessed through Amazon.com, 1986.

Remnick, David. *King of the World: Muhammad Ali and the Rise of an American Hero.* New York: Random House, 1998.

Rice, George Graham. *My Adventures with Your Money.* Las Vegas: Nevada Publications, 1986.

Riess, Steven A. "Gans, Joseph," in *American National Biography.* Edited by John A. Garraty and Mark C. Carnes. New York: Oxford University Press, 1999, 8: 678.

Rocap, William H., and Pember W. Rocap. *Remembering Bob Fitzsimmons.* Wayne, Maine: Archives Press, 2001.

Roosevelt, Theodore. *An Autobiography.* New York: Macmillan, 1913.

Rose, Al. *Eubie Blake.* New York: Schirmer, 1979.

Samuels, Charles. *The Magnificent Rube: The Life and Gaudy Times of Tex Rickard.* New York: McGraw-Hill, 1957.

Scharf, Thomas. *Images of Sports: Baltimore's Boxing Legacy 1893–2003.* Charleston, South Carolina: Arcadia, 2003.

Streible, Dan. *Fight Pictures: A History of Boxing and Early Cinema.* Berkeley: University of California Press, 2008.

Ward, Geoffrey C. *Unforgivable Blackness: The Rise and Fall of Jack Johnson.* New York: Alfred A. Knopf, 2004.

Webb, Dale. *Prize Fighter: The Life and Times of Bob Fitzsimmons.* Edinburgh and London: Mainstream Publishing, 2001.

Whitman, Walt. *Democratic Vistas.* The original edition in facsimile, Iowa Whitman Series, accessed through Amazon.com, 2009.

Zanjani, Sally. *The Glory Days in Goldfield, Nevada.* Reno and Las Vegas: University of Nevada Press, 2002.

———. *Goldfield: The Last Gold Rush on the Western Frontier.* Athens: Swallow Press of Ohio University Press, 1992.

———. *The Unspiked Rail: Memoir of a Nevada Rebel.* Reno: University of Nevada Press, 1981.

ACKNOWLEDGMENTS

I am grateful to my wife, Mary Fran, for her suggestions about this project, her ability to solve anything I thought was difficult about the work, and her patience. My children and their spouses responded every time I asked for their help in some way: Bill and Kelly, Dave and Stephanie, Maria and Chris, and Ann and Patrick. Mary Fran and I were blessed with three grandsons as the book progressed, giving us seven grandchildren in all.

There were others: longtime friends, and acquaintances whom I have gotten to know during the work. Ever since I met Tony Reid at *The Washington Post*, I have been impressed with his ideas, his editing, and his encouragement. I had him with me from the start of this, when he said, "Begin it in Goldfield." Paul Richard, Paul Hendrickson, and Shelby Coffey also dealt with the manuscript at various stages, and their advice seemed just right. Thank you: Henry Allen, Dwight Chapin, Jesse Coleman, Steve Conn, Lisa Crawley, Jerry Donovan, Molly Fessenden, Ben Forgey, Kevin Grace, David Hall, Dave Howell, Steve Lott, Bob Lyford, Karen Maine, Kathy Orton, Ed Padelford, Matt Schudel, Gary Schultz, David Sendler, Phil Smith, George Solomon, and Venlo Wolfsohn.

Andrew Blauner, my agent, took me to Farrar, Straus and Giroux. Paul Elie welcomed me and became my editor. How lucky can a person be? The two are pros.

INDEX